Still Rambling
AT SIXTY-NINE

AN ARCHAEOLOGIST'S MEMOIR

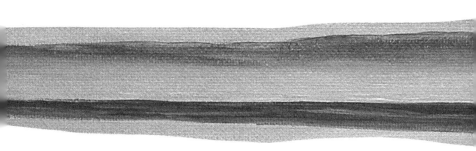

IAN W. BROWN

WITH A FOREWORD BY GEORGE C. RABLE

2021

Still Rambling at Sixty-Nine

An Archaeologist's Memoir

Ian W. Brown

ISBN 978-1734573091

BORGO
PUBLISHING

www.borgopublishing.com

Text and cover design: Borgo Publishing, Tuscaloosa, Alabama
Cover image: Painting by Georgia O'Keefe, *Lake George Study*, 1922,
courtesy of the Wiawaka Center for Women, Lake George, New York

Printed in the USA

For
The Elders

Contents

Foreword

WHAT YOU ARE ABOUT TO READ IS A REMARKABLE AND UNUSUAL piece of work. The title, *Still Rambling at Sixty-Nine: An Archaeologist's Memoir* is well chosen because Ian Brown has certainly written a memoir (of sorts), but the word "rambling" has at least two meanings here. Ian is still "rambling" of course (and probably a lot more as Covid restrictions abate), but this book "rambles" through his life. The "ramble" is not linear because this is not a typical memoir but rather a series of reflections not only about the author's past but about a host of questions, weighty and otherwise. Ian is neither wedded to chronology nor organization, and indeed within each chapter, he often digresses—and to good effect. Indeed, this unusual approach provides the reader with rich rewards.

Of course, we learn a great deal about Ian himself, but we also learn about family and friends along with much about the context of his life and times. He is an acute (and wry) observer of the natural, material, and human worlds. His powers of description and remarkable recall become immediately apparent in the semi-autobiographical short story, "Home." Here is the power of memory as well as reflections on childhood through fine descriptions of a house and property—what was back in the day and the changes that occurred over the years.

There is far less ego in these pages (except for his descriptions of early sports triumphs) than would be expected. Ian generally keeps his lamp well hidden under the proverbial bushel while fondly recalling many individuals who aided his journey. His wit is sly and sharp but never demeans other people and is often self-deprecating. As his friends can attest, Ian elevates rather than denigrates.

From the age of twelve, Ian Brown has kept a daily journal—a notable accomplishment in its own right; the regular process of writing has encouraged both reflection and attention to the rhythms of daily life. Consequently, he recognizes the value of introspective writing that both considers large questions while detailing smaller yet telling incidents. He lines up a Civil War play set, he burns trash, he does a single-day of yard work at a motel, and he spends summers on Lake George—all told in a way that unfailingly draws us into his life.

A man of broad interests, Ian systematically read through the Franklin Library classics in alphabetical order, all the while noting down his own reactions to the texts. Yet he wears such learning lightly even as he sprinkles his work with illuminating quotations from various authors. Ian early developed a passion for reading everything from comic books to mysteries to historical works (hence his willingness to hang out with historians). He lovingly describes how he has accumulated a large (and cumbersome to move) library over many years. He hunts for bargains, appreciates nicely bound tomes, carefully catalogs his collection, and gives a good number of books away (including the present volume).

Yet Ian does not embody the stereotypically detached intellectual; his "ramblings" always have a deeply human connection. His beloved wife Easty proves to be both anchor and occasional foil. Who cannot smile and be moved by the description of young daughter Avery cheering people up at a funeral? Or laugh at the accounts of restraining the always-on-the-move son Cabot? Ian confesses to being dead wrong about the interests his children would pursue, but his deep affection for his family permeates the book. Ian's own childhood to some degree sounds idyllic even as he presents his parents in ordinary scenes from home life but also as dance partners and travelers. His mother looms as a larger influence, and his slow-moving father is remembered with bemused affection. Ian fondly recalls colleagues and students always with an emphasis on their positive contributions to his life.

The role of popular culture receives insightful attention. Rather than listing movies and television shows that he either remembers best or enjoyed the most, Ian probes deeper to note the impact of at first limited and later expanded choices. The brief consideration of drive-in theaters is a real gem. Besides quoting memorable lines from films, he considers the wider impact of entertainment at various stages of life. Here as throughout the work, there is disarming candor as when Ian confesses to not having been greatly influenced by music at all.

Readers will learn a great deal about how Ian Brown came to be an archaeologist. A very early "dig" along with great enthusiasm for summer archaeological digs evolved into a lifelong interest in fieldwork across the world. He only briefly alludes to various foreign ventures that he has described in finer detail in several recent publications. His path to academia was uncertain and halting, but clearly the combination of museum work, teaching, and research served him well amidst the vicissitudes of the 1970s' tight job market and beyond. The attention to paths not taken and the role of randomness and timely contacts reveals a great deal about Ian's thoughtful approach to life and deep gratitude to colleagues and students. Even his list of likes and dislikes about 2020, a year of both pandemic and retirement that brought no small number of challenges and disappointments, shows a willingness to take advantage of adverse circumstances and displays Ian's remarkable work ethic.

However clichéd the phrase, Ian Brown has been a life-long learner. Working as a caddy taught him much about human nature. He has gained much through travel—including the wisdom of maintaining a leisurely pace and actually getting to know a place rather than passing through hurriedly with the next destination in mind. He has learned by not only asking questions—large and small—but by carefully considering them. This becomes especially evident in his wrestling with religious issues. And through this work, there is a becoming and genuine modesty, a recognition of limits to both knowledge and experience but a relentless drive to find meaning in life whether figuring out why he never cared for circuses or wrestling with the mystery of death. From the thoughtful introduction to the wonderful picture at the end, *Still Rambling* recounts a life well-remembered, well-recorded, and well-lived.

George C. Rable
Tuscaloosa, May 2021

Preface

I FIRMLY BELIEVE THAT ALL INDIVIDUALS CONSIDER THEMSELVES TO have some worth, but is there worth in a book about specific people if they have not made much of an impact on society? *The Diary of a Nobody* might be offered as affirmative to such, but it is fiction, a spoof originating in *Punch* Magazine.[1] If people write books about themselves, is the implication necessarily that they do so because they feel they are worthy of the attention? That seems to me to be putting on airs, and yet there is certainly nothing wrong with the practice of introspection, providing one does not bother others while doing it.

One thing's for sure, I have profited myself from the many years of putting words on paper and have enjoyed the process of placing before you some of my ramblings. There are two main questions offered in *Sophie's World*: "Who are you?" and "Where does the world come from?"[2] I do not care all that much as to the latter conundrum, where the world came from, and where it will be a billion years from now also matters little to me. I will leave these questions to creationists and the evolutionists, two sets of scholars who are far more curious and abler than me to resolve. I do, however, have some concern for who I am and why I am here, more than enough of a puzzle to have kept me up at night on more than one occasion.

---

1 George and Weedon Grossmith, *The Diary of a Nobody* (London: The Folio Society, 2016).

2 Jostein Gaarder (Trans. Paulette Moller), *Sophie's World, a Novel about the History of Philosophy* (London: The Folio Society, 2019).

I first started to think of such matters in 1959 when walking through a cemetery in England. I was seven years old at the time and was fascinated by the gravestones I saw before me. Names were given on each marker, as were dates of birth and death. Many had epitaphs as well, but that provided little satisfaction to a curious child who wanted to know who exactly all these people were. Also in that same year a Boy Scout group where I grew up did some excavations at a nearby Colonial Inn outside Albany, New York and I was invited to participate. The inn had disappeared at least a century or two by the time I had my first archaeological experience, but its footprint was still visible in the Pine Bush area west of the city. Looking back, the work was clearly an amateurish affair, as we youngsters were allowed to keep whatever artifacts we found. At the time that seemed to be a perfectly legitimate ruling of the scout-master and I would have been quite disappointed had it been otherwise. I myself went home with a cigar box full of rusty old nails and a small brass candelabrum that was melted into a mangled shape. Periodically while growing up I would re-move that object from the box and wonder who owned it, who carried it, what was their trade, their beliefs, their joys, and their woes? If only that person had written a book.

This is not a self-help book. It is not a tell-all book. And it is certainly not of great worth to anyone who might want to learn all that much about the great and interesting people that I have met along the way. They are in here, to be sure, but I tell more of me than I do of them. As per Thoreau, "I should not talk so much about myself if there were anybody else whom I knew so well. Unfortunately, I am confined to this theme by the narrowness of my experience."[3] That may not be to the liking of readers who want to see well beyond me and my life, but

---

3 Henry D. Thoreau, *Walden, or Life in the Woods* (Franklin Center, Pennsylvania: The Franklin Library, 1976), 2.

I make no apologies. As my existence goes forward, my eyes constantly stare into the past, a practice that gives me perspective if not wisdom. Montaigne said it far more eloquently than me, "Let childhood look ahead, old age backward: was not this the meaning of the double face of Janus? Let the years drag me along if they will, but backward. As long as my eyes can discern that lovely season now expired, I turn them in that direction at intervals. If youth is escaping from my blood and my veins, at least I want not to uproot the picture of it from my memory."[4]

Still Rambling at Sixty-Nine consists of 16 ramblings on a variety of subjects with the first account being a fledgling attempt at a short story. "Home" is indeed based on my youth, but it is enhanced by (suffers from?) artistic license. Many of the other essays were composed in concert with three good friends—Guy Ward Hubbs, Lawrence Frederick Kohl, and George C. Rable. We four academicians, three historians and an archaeologist, have known each other for several decades. Each Wednesday for many years we have gathered together for breakfast simply to enjoy each other's company and to deliberate upon the inanities of the world. In recent times our group came to be known as "The Elders" not only because that is what we ourselves have become, but because of our tendency to pontificate on a variety of topics whenever we meet and then not do anything about it. We consider ourselves to be absolutely impeccable authorities, at least among ourselves.

One day early in 2019 Elder Rable decided to share an essay with us that he wrote on "The Books That Built Me."[5] This stimulated a response from the others that generated a flurry

---

4 Michel de Montaigne (Trans. Donald M. Frame), *Essays* (Franklin Center, Pennsylvania: The Franklin Library 1980), 412.
5 George C. Rable "The Books That Built Me," *The Civil War Monitor* (2019 Spring): 70-71.

of discussion for well over a year on a multitude of topics, including books, movies, television, music, religion, reunions, travel, and much more. In the space of 16 months we learned a great deal about each other that was new and often surprising. I assembled and edited our combined essays and email messages into a manuscript that I called "By and For the Elders," which was shared among the four of us. Although greatly appreciated, or so they said, there was majority concurrence among the authors that their various writings and responses would remain private. One member of the group, me, felt otherwise and so I offer most of my essays here as a series of ramblings.

I have never felt that my life is or should be an open book, but I really have said nothing within this volume that I am ashamed to reveal (I don't think), and hope upon hope that by voicing my views and opinions I have not hurt anyone in the process. If so, I apologize profusely and blame my transgressions on the advancing age of an archaeologist.

Home

(A SHORT STORY)

He leaned against the car and gazed upon the house. How small it looked. The yard before it, which led at a slight incline up to the house, looked diminished in size too, at least from how he remembered it. Had it been spring the lawn would have been awash with the brilliant colors of phlox, purple blooms mostly, but those had long since gone, picked out by an overzealous aunt who could not distinguish between beauty and weed. The rock garden was still there, as was the cedar bush, now a large healthy tree which overpowered the house. The concrete steps, two in all, led up to a centrally placed doorway, with a double window on the right and a single one on the left, living room and master bedroom respectively, or at least that is what they once were. He laughed to himself. "Master" truly seems an inappropriate term, because a queen-sized bed would have more than filled the space. It was a bedroom, pure and simple. A girl and a boy stood on the steps in Easter clothing, the girl maybe nine or 10 and the boy seven, if that. She had a dainty bonnet on her head and he a jaunty fedora, all spiffed up for religion. A small boy, maybe three, came running around the left side of the building with a look of terror on his face. He held in his hand a paint brush, dripping white. As he passed the steps and headed to the tree a middle-aged man, maybe 40ish, chased him down. He was desperate to get that brush away from the mischievous lad. The house was red you see, and the brush was not, so the explanation for the fuss was obvious. He smiled at the happenings.

"Can I help you?" said a woman.

He was startled. She came from his right carrying a load of groceries. She was in her late 40s, maybe 50, about a decade younger than him. She was of medium build and good looking, at least to his eyes, but not what one would really call pretty. Just nice. She had short brown hair, which was covered by a yellow scarf and wore a light brown coat, perfect for a cool October day.

"Oh, I'm sorry. I didn't see you turn into the driveway. Yes, I mean no, you can't help me. I actually should be helping you. Carry the groceries I mean. I can't imagine what you must think of me standing here staring at your home. I mean, it is your home isn't it?"

She smiled, "Do you want to buy it? We're putting it on the market but haven't put the sign up. Have you talked to our realtor?"

"No, I didn't know it was for sale."

The woman hesitated. She had never seen this man before and here he was staring at her home, but with no interest in buying. She knew he was not from around here, as she had never seen him before, though his looks were slightly familiar—something in her past.

"I'm from around here," the man said, "or at least I used to be. I grew up in your house. My name is Ian, Ian Brown. I'm Winnie and Bill Brown's son."

She smiled. "Bill Brown…yes, now I know why you look familiar. He was such a fine man. You know you look just like him. He made me laugh so."

"They always remember Dad," he thought to himself.

"Were you living here when we bought the house?" she asked.

"No, I had moved down south. This is the first time I've been back."

"Why, that 25 years ago! You haven't been home since?"

"To the area yes, once or twice to high school reunions, but not to my home."

They talked awhile longer. She asked about his Mom and Dad and was sad to learn that they had both passed. As she shuffled the bag of groceries from one hand to other, he said, "Please let me carry that for you."

She gave him the bag, which had now become very heavy, and asked, "Would you like to come in?"

He was a little hesitant because he didn't want to intrude, but he also wanted to see inside, to see if the interior had changed any. The outside hadn't altered much, so maybe everything else had remained the same too. He followed her up the driveway and entered the breezeway, which filled the space between the house and the garage. As she opened the door, she hesitated, and he did too. She seemed nervous, and rightfully so. She did not know the man and she was alone. He instantly picked up on the tension.

"Would you like to see something that you've never noticed before?" he asked.

"Okay, I guess." She looked at him confusedly. He might have asked if she wanted to dance as to how curious the statement was, but he had good gentle eyes and she trusted him.

He walked to the back of the breezeway and showed her a spot on the wall, which once had served as the outside wall of the garage. The wall had been painted many times in the past, but still visible, barely visible, was a column of four dots, each placed an inch or so above the other. "See this? Do you want to guess?"

She bent down a little and scratched her head. I have absolutely no idea. How in lord's name did you know those dots were there?"

"It's easy. The lowest one is 12, the next one is 13, and so on up to 16. It's my height, measured each year at the same time. I stopped around 5 foot 8 and that was that, truly one of the disappointments of my life. Four inches more and I might have played basketball in college." He laughed. "Well, probably not, but I like to kid myself at times."

She smiled and was more comfortable now. "You really did live here, didn't you? Imagine, a column of dots can tell so much once you have the explanation. I must have seen them before, but they never registered with me. Come on inside." Mounting a second set of stairs, which was once the side door to the house, he looked to its right. There was still a slight shadow on the wall where the milk box used to be. So many shadows. Once in the house he gasped. "Where's the kitchen?!" It should have been right there. As soon as the door opened it would have hit Dad's chair. Around the small table nestled against the wall was, in clockwise order, Dad's chair, Ian's chair, Jennifer's chair, and then Mom's chair, right beneath the phone that was mounted on the wall. She controlled the phone—and no calls at dinner time! Tweetie-Bird, the last in a long line of feathered pets, swung from a small cage above the window, but now there was no window, no phone, no table, just a large open space. A hook in the ceiling, which once supported the cage, now held a planter bearing a lush green begonia spotted with small red flowers. Same object, different function.

"Oh, we opened up this area 20 years ago," the woman said. "I don't know how your parents managed in such a small space."

The man smiled, because he didn't know either. And it wasn't just parents. This is where everyone ate, even relatives from England who would visit and stay for a year or two. Somehow Mom juggled all the various foods into meals in the miniscule space available to her, the real miracles being Thanksgiving, Christmas, and Easter, when feasts were prepared and served for half a dozen people, and even more at times.

"Yes, we knocked out the back wall soon after we got here. We had two children after all, and this tiny house just couldn't accommodate our needs."

He smiled. To a child this home was absolutely gigantic, but how our views have changed in time. He looked to the left of the door into the living room. A small boy, the same one that he had seen earlier, who had been running as fast as his chubby little legs could carry him, stood at the window peering out between the thick venetian blinds. He had curly blonde hair, wore shorts, and had suspenders—Good Lord—suspenders! He turned around, looked at the man, and moaned. He had a tear in his eye. "Jebba's gone," he said softly, and then looked back through the window. "Jebba's gone."

The man walked to his side and glanced out the window. To the right, up the hill, he saw the rear end of a school bus just making a turn around the neighborhood. The man knew it would shortly loop back, but the boy did not. How could he know? The world was just too large outside his home. He had no clue where the bus went and the minute or two that passed was an eternity. "Here it comes!" Jebba waved from the window and he knew that wherever it was going he was not included.

The man peered around the small room. All had changed except the space itself. It was loaded with boxes now because the woman was packing. There were still enough furnishings in place for him to realize that the "new" occupants had a very different sense of style than had his parents. But there was still one piece of furniture that he thought he recognized, an old red couch with a raised texture that swirled into a complex design. For most of the time that he lived at home the couch bore a slipcover, presumably because Mom was embarrassed by its age. It was a product of the 1940s, probably a handy-me-down from Aunt Madge and Uncle Bert. Maybe, but he wasn't sure of that. Who knows just how one ends up with the things that surround you? The man noticed a baby lying on its back staring at the couch. It was clear that the child was unaware of him, as he couldn't see into the distance. He was just too young, so he simply lay there staring. Then his pudgy little finger reached up and started to follow the outline of the design, slowly but surely associating touch with memory.

"Are you okay?"

"Yes, I was just thinking how much things have changed in the house. I hardly recognize the place now."

"Well, it has been a quarter of a century. We raised our children here, but they're gone now. One is married and the other in school. Time flies, eh? We're moving to a larger home. You see my husband will be retiring in a few years and this was only going to be a starter-home for us anyway." She laughed, "A starter-home and our kids have not known anything different."

He didn't answer, but the term did take him aback. Starter-home. That's how his Mom and Dad must have thought about it too. This tiny little place, which was his nest, his home, was probably only considered a place to start, a place to raise two children through their early education, and then move on, as they did. "Thankfully, they never mentioned that to me," he mused.

"Would you like to see more of the place?" she asked. She was no longer wary to be in the home with him alone, a stranger, and he really did want to see the rest of the place, not so much to be shocked by changes, but to see if there were any vestiges of the past that remained, the hidden niches of concealment whose meanings were only evident to those who stacked memories within them.

He followed her through the living room into a very small hall. On one side was the miniscule bathroom, which looked out into the back yard, on the other side the master bedroom, and straight ahead was the guest bedroom, which had served as his own space for most of his early years. Not until Jennifer graduated from high school was he able to move upstairs to the "big" bedroom. As they entered the hall, he resisted the temptation to jump up and grab the trim of the door, the little ledge that served as a swing for a 14-year old boy full of vim and vigor. "Get off that! The whole thing will come tumbling down!" Mom would protest. It never did of course, but she was probably more concerned with the fingerprints that she had to wash, because lord knows we can't have any of those. He laughed to himself and then looked up.

"Did you ever notice that?" he asked. A small square hole, no larger than the shoulders of a slender man was positioned in the middle of the ceiling, outlined with the same trim that edged the wall.

"Yes, but we could never figure out what it is, or was. It looks like it might have been a trapdoor, but what would be the purpose, as it simply leads into the upstairs bedroom?"

"Ah, but not always. Once it led to Christmas."

She laughed, "Okay, explain."

"When I was a boy, I saw my Dad climb up into that hole and come down with a small tree. My Mom took it from him and placed some small ornaments on it. She put it on a table in the living room and placed around it boxes from my relatives in England. Always on Christmas Eve we got to open these gifts from grandmas, granddads, aunts and uncles. Dad always got homemade socks and handkerchiefs, and Jebba and I always had Rountree's Aero chocolate bars. And it all started with the opening of that little trapdoor."

She still looked puzzled. "But it leads into the upstairs bedroom."

"Not always. It really did once lead into the attic, though I didn't realize that until later. The upstairs bedroom was an addition, constructed by my Dad and Grandfather, my Mom's Dad, when I was about two. Just as you and your husband felt the need to extend the back of the house to make a kitchen and larger dining area, my Dad knocked out the wall over the cellar stairwell and built upwards." He pointed down the hall, "My sister and I once shared the guestroom, which was hardly big enough to house one child, never mind two."

"You are my sunshine, my only sunshine. You make me happy when skies are gray..."

"Where's that coming from?" he asked.

"Where's what coming from?"

"The music. The singing."

"I don't hear it."

"I imagine you hear other things," he said.

Now she seemed a little worried. "I really don't hear anything."

"Oh, but your children probably will. Hear things I mean." The moment he said this the curly-haired blonde boy ran by him and hustled up the stairs as fast as his little legs would carry him. And then, just as quickly, he descended the stairs carrying an imaginary burden. "Here's your pie Granddad." An old man, in his late 60s, sat before a little box in the living room watching the New York Yankees playing the Brooklyn Dodgers. "Well where have you been Laddie and what have you brought me?" he asked. "It's a cherry pie from Cherry Valley," said the lad proudly. "Oh my, oh my, what a grand pie that is. Sit upon my lap and I shall sing to thee. Are ye ready? Well then, I love to go a-wandering along the mountain track, and as I go, I love to sing, my knapsack on my back. Val-deri, val-dera, val-deri, val-dera. Ha, ha, ha, ha, ha, ha. Ha! Val-dera! My knapsack on my back." They then snuggled and both eyes wandered back to the magic box. Baseball was stupid, but soon it would be "Howdy Doody Time." Jebba would be home then and together they would curl up in the chair and, from the vantage of their 'peanut gallery' would be enamored by the antics of Buffalo Bob and Clarabell the Clown.

"May I take a peek into your guest bedroom," the man asked.

"Certainly, but I think you might be a little disappointed."

She was correct. He was disappointed, as the room no longer served as such. He had expected to see a large drum set at the base of a small bed, the only spot in the house where he was permitted to pound away on it. The room was now used as a "gym", but not much of one at that, as it could only accommodate a running machine. Like most home exercise equipment, it clearly was seldom used, as several boxes were piled on the track and a freshly laundered shirt hung on a hanger from the handlebars. She laughed, "We get as much exercise from moving the damn thing around as we ever did from turning it on!"

He peered out the window. The creek was still there, which he always pronounced "crick" in his youth. He couldn't see it though, as the vegetation was thick, but he could still hear it as the window was open. Once the area leading down to it would have looked like a neat, little English park. A man stood out there with his ax and beside him was what appeared to be yet another boy, 10 or so, maybe older. They were engaged in some sort of argument. The man looked worried as the boy persisted. Finally, he gently pushed the boy to the side and lifted the ax high above his head. It came down in a rapid arc at the base of a small tree. He did it several more times, as the boy looked on, eager with anticipation. The man gave him the handle, said a few more words of warning, and stepped back. The boy proceeded to follow the pattern of his father and swung the ax. The first stroke was tentative and though it hit its mark, it made no significant dent on the tree. The next stroke was stronger and more determined, and chips started to fly. After five or six strokes the tree snapped in two and the lad looked so proud. His father did too, and actually seemed a bit surprised. "Now run along he said. You can do some more later."

"You sure do get distracted," she said with amusement.

"I'm so sorry. Just looking at ghosts."

"Well, let me show you a few others. The upstairs and basement are loaded with them, or at least that's what the kids say!"

"I'll forgo the attic he said," shaking his head. He remembered the nasty game that his sister and friends played, hiding upstairs in the dark and calling his name. How excited he was to be included. The first hand that reached out from under the bed and grabbed his ankle was more than enough to send him running to Mom. At least they got scolded for that, but he still remembered.

They returned to what had been the kitchen and opened the cellar door. Some things never do change it seems. Twelve wooden steps. He didn't need to count as he knew them by heart. When he was small it was one at a time, but by age 16 he could do the jump, either up or down, four at a time. Now, with his aged bones, he was back to one step at a time.

The wall on the left had a sliding door over it. "Canned goods?" he asked.

"Why yes, how did you know?"

"What else could it be?" he laughed. "The outside door leads directly to the cellar, so if I weren't here you probably would have carried that bag of yours right down the stairs."

"Yes, you do know this house, don't you?"

"When you know so much about it, it's a home. And perhaps I know something of human nature too." Then he laughed to himself. Dad always used the phrase "human nature" to describe or rationalize what he himself did or believed, and when he referred to what the "common man" thinks or does, he was always talking about himself. "Why would Dad want to be common," he mused, remembering that to his mother to be common was the worst possible insult she could apply to a person, especially in reference to another woman! To be common is, well, we are not that kind of people!

At the bottom of the stairs he turned and looked up, expecting to see the old tennis racket, and by God, it was still there! "I can't believe it," he said, "the racket is still there."

"Do you know anything about it? We left it there because it just seemed to belong in that spot."

"Yes, it does, and no, I know nothing about it, beyond coming to the realization one day that it must have been either my mother's or father's." The man just couldn't fathom that Mom and Dad once played tennis. This would imply that they were young once, but to children parents are never young. Simply becoming a parent changes your age and becoming a grandparent makes you old beyond your years.

The sound of a bottle spinning in the other room caught his attention. There were giggles and he immediately knew what was going on. The woman apparently did not hear it, as she had already turned the corner to reset the dryer. Two of the children, clearly teens, one male one female, rushed by her and sat on the washer. They laughed, kissed, and laughed once more. Two young children gazed in through the window from the dark outside. They held hands and laughed too, knowing full well what the future would bring for them as well. The man sighed, which spoiled everything, because the children thought they were alone.

"You sighed?" the woman asked.

"Nothing," he said, "Just a happy memory. I have many."

His hand fell upon the cinderblock column beside him. It

was rough to the touch. Once it was gray, but seven decades of life in the cellar tarnished it and produced a blackish hue. Within it was ductwork that carried hot air from the oil furnace to the rooms above. A little rectangular door, perhaps six by three inches, existed halfway up, its purpose curious and unknown. "Santa comes out right there," the man said.

"What?!"

"Santa. He comes out of there with his large bag of toys. There is no fireplace in this home, as you well know, so Santa has to come out of the chimney someplace—sister Jebba says."

"Maybe we ought to go upstairs."

"What, no drink from the bar?"

Even she had to laugh at that. "Do you know, we never used it. In fact, I don't ever think we have even entertained guests down here. Whoever would have installed a bar in this depressing place?"

He disagreed with her analysis of it being a depressing place but had to admit that the bar itself was strange. "It was a 1960s kind of thing to do," he said, "but, ironically, neither my mother nor father drank spirits. All of the bottles that were on the shelves were filled with colored water. Bombay Sapphire gin has never looked so blue!" They both laughed at that.

"Look there," he said. "See the stain on the wall? That comes from making volcanos." She looked confused, so he continued. "Vinegar, baking soda, and dish detergent. Makes for quite an explosion, especially if you use too much baking soda."

"Okay..." she said, "Was chemistry your forte?"

"Not exactly, but I did have a pretty functional chemistry set, and to complete it my Dad gave me a test tube full of mercury. He said to be very careful though, because if I spilled it, it would be a devil to pick up. And that was true. It emptied on to the floor one day and it took me almost an hour to gather up the pellets and get them back into the tube."

"Mercury?"

"Yes. It was a different time. I think he might have told me to be sure not to eat it, but that would have been pretty much the same with anything he had down here. This was his workshop you see. I used to play basketball in it."

"What do you mean?"

"Well, I loved the game. I had a ball and I had a hoop, both of which I got for Christmas. The only thing missing was a court, so I set up the hoop in this vise and swish! I could make a basket from anywhere in the cellar."

"But there wasn't a backboard?"

"Nope. Didn't need one, though admittedly, when I did miss it wreaked havoc with the cabinet of screws. My father wasn't too happy, so when the weather warmed up, he built me a small blacktop court in the backyard. He did make a mistake though. By attaching the hoop to the back of the garage every time I played the house rocked."

"I can imagine," she said. "Would you like to see what the backyard looks like now?"

He was reluctant to leave the cellar, what with Valerie sitting on the washer beckoning him, but he was now far too old for her, too old in fact for any of the ghosts that still inhabited the house. As he reached the top of the stairs, he half expected to see his Mom preparing a banana sandwich for him or Dad busily studying his stamps. "Hey Ian, did you know that the Penny Black is the oldest stamp in the world?"

"No Dad, didn't know that." And could have finished with, "and couldn't care less..." but that would have been cruel. Right now he wished he could sit beside him and learn all about the Penny Black and why it was so very important.

"Come on outside," she encouraged. She led him through the unfamiliar room that had been added by them to his home

and they went out into the yard. There were leaves everywhere, as autumn was well on its way.

"I sure remember these!" he said.

"Yes, it does take some raking."

"My father did not rest easily until every leaf was picked
up. He would go over it again and again until it was immacu-
late." He paused, "It would drive me absolutely crazy."

"My husband isn't like that."

"Lucky you," he said. "I picked up a lot of things from my
Dad, but anal retentiveness wasn't one of them...I don't think."
He remembered just how carefully he catalogs each and every
one of his book purchases and how they are organized first by
topic and then alphabetically. And when he reads them, how
he must always write a review or an evaluation so as to recollect them when needed.

He changed the subject, "You know, it's not quite filled in."

"What isn't?"

"The hole in the ground. See? On the lawn over there before you head into the woods and down to the crick."

She didn't see what he meant, so he pointed out how the
descending sun was leaving a shadow on the grass. With each
minute that passed a large slightly off-color round patch was
coming to light.

"What is it?" she asked.

"It's a hole. A big hole in fact. My father killed a giant black
snake in that hole. He took a hoe and chopped off his big head.
Poisonous no doubt, or at least that's what my sister said." But
now he began to wonder. How earnestly he trusted whatever
Jebba said. "In any event, it was a snake. And it came up from
the crick via a big gully."

Yes, that gully had to be filled. Just as his father had tamed
the wilderness by clearing out timber and underbrush that
grew by the water, he had to fight back that growing abyss that

was bringing serpents into our backyard. He was aided by the large tree that fell, the one that he slowly but surely cut up into pieces, all carefully stacked within the gully, and of course the seasonal deposition of leaves contributed. Jackie helped with the tree cutting and Janet, the girl next door, the one whose hand was held, helped with the leaves. Who could ask for better friends?

"I can see them still," he said.

"See who?"

"Three children lying over there in the gulley covered with leaves of yellow and red. You don't see them? Each of them is lying flat on their backs looking up at the sky, wondering, just wondering."

He turned around and pointed at the rubble of old cinder blocks. "That's where I became what I am," he said. The pile was only a couple of feet high and the blocks were just barely intact. They resembled cubes of sugar sitting in water just before they dissolved. "Once that pile was five or six feet tall, the carefully saved foundation blocks for a future garage. The garage was eventually built, but by that time the cinderblocks were no good. My father didn't remove them because it was quite possible that that dastardly snake came from there."

"Well, you then were brave to sit on them."

"Not really. We never believed in the myth of the Great Snake, despite what Jebba said."

"What do you mean when you said that's where you became what you are?"

"Jackie asked me what I was going to be, and I said, 'an archaeologist.' I couldn't have been more than seven or eight years old. Earlier in the summer a Boy Scout leader, a friend of the family, asked if I wanted to join his troop and dig for a day. Would I ever! We excavated at an 18th-century inn, probably illegally, but I didn't know that at the time." He laughed, "Yes, you can be sure it was professional because we got to keep what we found."

"Find anything good."

"I actually did. I found a brass candlestick holder, which was all crushed into a clump. I kept it in a cigar box in the cellar and would bring it out periodically just to hold it. I could imagine myself climbing the stairs of that old inn with the candelabrum in hand, wondering if there were Indians outside who were stalking the place. How could one not become an archaeologist with those kinds of thoughts?"

He pointed back towards the woods at the corner of the yard and said, "Asparagus."

"Okay?" She looked at him kind of funny. "Asparagus?"

"That was the corner of the vegetable garden. Dad planted corn and asparagus, probably other things too, but that's all I remember." They walked over to the woods and saw a large clump of curious looking grass.

"I've never noticed that before. How do you know it's asparagus?"

"It has spear-shaped ends, even after all these years. When I was a child it had already gone to seed. I don't think we ever got a crop out of it, or anything else out of the garden for that matter. My Dad could maintain a lawn, but vegetable gardens just weren't his thing?"

The old barbecue was still there at the end of the yard. "My father and Granddad built that." It was a solid structure made of river cobbles. "They tried to move it once, to get it away from the parking lot for the Grove, but it started to fall apart. They just left it there and I myself never even remember it being used."

"What's a Grove?" she asked.

"For most of the last century, especially in the middle half, that was a place where people from the city came to enjoy themselves. There was a large outdoor pool, and lots of buildings large and small for weddings, banquets, and various activities. Clambakes. I remember there used to be lots of clambakes, even in the 1950s when I was a child. They stopped though, or at least became rarer sometime in the next decade. I think television might have had something to do with it. People weren't getting together quite so much. Kind of sad really."

"Do you want to go back in the house again? Maybe a cup of coffee?"

"No, I must get going. But thank you. It was really nice of you to take the time to show me around my home."

"And it was nice of you to show me things that I had never noticed before, but now I will."

He smiled, "I bet you could show me a lifetime of things in your memory that I wouldn't recognize for what they are."

"Yes, I bet I could, but I just haven't recognized them yet," she said.

"Do you mind if I just walk around the side of the house alone? I can get to my car from there."

"No problem. It was really nice meeting you Mr. Brown. You know, you really are a lot like your father." He shook his head no, but she insisted, "No, you really are. You're a very nice man. A little strange," she said, "but in a nice way. Come back anytime."

"Thanks. Maybe I will when I get old."

She waved at him as he turned the corner of the house. He picked up the brush from the bucket and applied one stroke on the wall. That was all that was needed. He then gingerly stepped from one stone to the next along the top of the rock garden as he made his way to the front of the house, just as he had done a thousand times before. "I could do this in my dreams" he thought. "I wonder if this was all a dream anyway."

He drove his car to the top of the hill, passed Jackie Clark's house and turned left at Milt Kranz's. Just after Denny Richardson's house he turned right into what had once been a dirt driveway. This had been an old farmhouse once, owned by old Mrs. Knowles. She was a witch, or at least Janet and he thought she was. In the distance he saw Janet sitting next to a young lad on the roof of one of the old buildings. Mrs. Knowles was heading toward them with what looked like a knife in her hand and screaming, "Get off of there! You'll be killed." They scurried off, laughing excitedly as they scurried to the safety of their respective homes, side by side nestled against the crick that harbored snakes.

He laughed to himself. Old Mrs. Knowles. She must have been 60, if that, but she had gray hair, so she was ancient.

This was her home, he thought. This held her memories. This held her youth. The home was gone, torn down in the summer of 1970, just after he started college. He visited it then after reading an article in the newspaper. People were sad to see it go, but Mrs. Knowles had died and the roof leaked badly, so no one wanted to live in it. Plus, kids were looking in the windows and breaking in. If they didn't tear it down, it would probably burn down. Excavations were planned they said, as if materials could ever tell all. They were clues, but without someone there to tell what things meant, they make no sense. He thought of the brass candelabrum that he had found at the old inn and said aloud, "Well, at least it's something. Something to make sense of the ghosts."

Early Work

WORK COMES IN ALL FLAVORS, BUT WHAT I AM REFERRING TO HERE is paid employment. I am certain I thought about such matters early on in life, from watching my mother count money and pay bills, but like most people I have little beyond memory to demonstrate this is true. Confirmation that I did indeed have thoughts of earning a living comes from my first diary (1964) when I was 12 years old. From Day 2 of that year I was involved in fiscal endeavors.

January 2—It snowed today so Steven and I went shoveling driveways and earned $1.50. I spent 15 cents of it to get cocoa and candy. Later we played WWII with his train. At night we removed the presents from our tree.

January 12—This morning after I went to Sunday school I worked on my timeline for Social Studies. Later Uncle Bernard came and I earned $2.50 cleaning his shop. When I got home I got some ski boots for $6.00. At night I thought there was a burglar in the house.

January 14—Today because of the Blizzard they canceled school. I went out shoveling driveways. I did two and earned $4.50. $2.50 were in pennies for my coin collection. We were trying to arrange a combo band. Later Steven came over and we played games.

January 26—Today I went to church and sang in the choir. When I got home I ate and then went to work at my uncle's shop. I earned $5.00 because he didn't pay me last week. At night I studied for my math test and then watched "Grindl."

January 28—Today I had my science test and missed nine out of 100 questions. When I got home it was snowing real hard so my sister went skiing and I shoveled snow. I earned $1.50 from Mrs. Reed. At night I watched Tues. night movie.

My diary stopped on February 11, no doubt because of boredom, but it picked up again when school let out in June.

July 11—Today I got up, watched T.V., and then ate breakfast. The Twins played Pitch for awhile and then Mr. Dibelo took us down to the beach. I helped with [swimming] lessons today and then jumped in for the Ti and earned $1.08. Whenever I dive now, my head hurts just above my eyes. At night, Jo, Jill, Sharon, Corky, Jennifer, Alan, Kathleen and I went to see "What a way to go."

At the end of my 1964 diary there were pages to record monthly cash accounts. I attach here the

Cash Account—January	Received		Paid	
shoveling	1	50		15
bowling			1	85
allowance		35		
shop	2	50		
ski boots			6	00
shoveling	4	50		
shop	5	00		
wood off			8	30
shoveling	1	50		
mess	1	00		
	16	35	8	30

My Financial Statement for January 1964.

month of January in order to provide a sample as to what I received and what I paid out. My earnings of $16.35 and expenditures of $8.30 demonstrate that I was certainly on the right track with regard to a life of financial integrity.

The above entries really do match my memory. Shoveling snow, helping to clean my aunt and uncle's beauty salon (each and every Sunday), and diving for money were three methods of making money. I will get back to the "Ti" shortly, as that was a summer activity, but starting first in and around my Albany home, I imagine that my initial job was an allowance from parents. I sought things to do and my Mom and Dad sought to keep me alive while I was doing them. For example, mowing the lawn was *verboten* until I could convince them that I would not slice my foot off. Cleaning the bird cage, however, was good and safe. My mother had a string of canaries and parakeets over the years and even though there was only one of them at a time, the mess was enough to convince me that caged creatures were indeed a bad thing. Another chore involved people trash. There was an expression when I was a child that often led to a fight—"Make me!" and the artful retort was, "I don't make trash. I burn it." In my case, that was true. The refuse created by my family, including me, was "made" and subsequently deposited in the back yard. My job, which I did for all the time that I lived at home (basically when I went off to college), was to cart the trash outside, dump it into an empty oil can, and burn it. I don't remember composting anything we threw away, so I'm not exactly sure just how I got it to burn. Periodically my father would upend the can and dump the debris into a slowly filling gully. My family's life, in material terms, is contained in that gully and I suppose an archaeologist of the future could excavate it and learn much about the dietary behavior of the Brown's. In the future only those who live in rural areas can contribute toward this kind of study, as garbage pickup and recycling have truncated an important part of the story.

In addition to snow shoveling, I remember selling Christmas cards year after year. From that enterprise I received merchandise, not money. I only remember two items, a pup tent and a pair of water skis. The tent lacked a floor, so it was useless, and the skis were an embarrassment when I finally did learn to water ski and saw what others were using. So much for selling Christmas cards.

I desperately wanted a newspaper route. Some friends of mine had ones and I would help them periodically. Although they would give me some chump change so that I would keep coming back, I mostly did it because I was bored and could hang out with buddies. As for me having my own route, my Mom and Dad said, "Absolutely not!" I don't remember if they gave me an explanation that settled well with me, but looking back from the perspective of a parent I could imagine what my father must have said to my mother—"What happens if Ian gets sick?" My father sure didn't want a paper route to add to his already full day, but sickness or not, papers would still have had to be delivered. My mother sure wasn't going to do it! A happy consequence of not having a paper route is that I have always had a great love for dogs.

There were no other money-paying jobs that I can remember in my life at home. I played high school soccer and basketball which, between practice and games, gave me no extra time. Let me correct that. The extra time that I did have was consumed by eating, studying and the never-ending pursuit of girls.

Work really began in a serious manner once I went up to Lake George in the Adirondacks in the summer. Our home was a small trailer, which we used on weekends. Eventually, as I grew older and more responsible, I stayed in the trailer for the whole summer. I think I must have been 15 when my older sister, who was doing maid service at a motel, asked me if I wanted to do yard work for the place. Knowing my antipathy to gardening of any sort, it's hard to believe I said yes. I have mowed, weeded, and cursed extraneous vegetation for most of my adult life (until I had enough money to hire others to do it for me), but I've never been happy about it. Nevertheless, I did tell my sister yes, and one June morning showed up at the motel ready to work. My boss gave me some gloves and some clippers and told me to trim the errant grass sticking out of the stone wall that circled the entrance to the establishment. Before completing the tale of my foray into the gardening world, I should make mention of what June is like in the Adirondacks. That's when the No-See-Ums come out. Mosquitomagnet.com describes them as follows, "No-See-Ums are tiny, biting insects that can be a plague to many communities. Particularly prevalent in coastal areas, No-See-Ums are often just as much of a pest as mosquitoes. They can ruin outdoor get-togethers, make a round of golf intolerable and devastate your vacation plans." They can also drive a young boy mad, the result being me quitting my first real job after only one day. I didn't actually quit; I just didn't return, thus sacrificing a few dollars duly earned to ward off personal embarrassment. I did have (and still do have) some guilt for my behavior, but a week of flicking my ears while asleep convinced me that I had indeed made the right decision.

With gardening out, caddying was in. It certainly was a more pleasant and lucrative substitute. At least I thought it would be. The park where we kept our trailer for a decade or so, at first called Scenic Farm Park and later Scenic View Campground, was perched midway up a small, gentle mountain. On the top of the mountain was the golf course for the famous Sagamore Hotel, which was located on Green Island adjacent to the village of Bolton Landing. Each day I would get up at dawn and march through the woods and up the hill (I really do find it difficult to call it a mountain) to the golf course. At the time the course was in need of repair, but now it is a world class establishment with green fees far beyond my means, if I even cared that is. One perk of being a caddy was that I could play the course after 6 p.m., so I did take advantage of that all through the summer of 1967.

The way that I got the job of being a caddy was to just show up; and I did, religiously so, along with a dozen other boys of about my age. The key to going out with a golfer was to be the pet of the Pro. I can't remember his name, but he was a short, thin, balding man with a large red birthmark on his skull. He was mad all the time, or so it seemed, and his caddies received the brunt of it. There were no golf carts in those days, at least at this club, so the Pro needed to have a slew of caddies around at all times, but he sure didn't like us. There were only a few that were his favorites, and they inevitably showed up each and every day. Many an hour I sat there with the others waiting to be called. We pitched pennies, told tall tales of sexual exploits, and did our fair share of cursing and spitting. The best chance of getting called was if the day was gloomy and rain was probable. Only then were the caddy numbers down, so the chances of heading off with a bag were improved. One bag earned me $3 and a $1 tip if the golfer was pleased with me. Two bags got me $8, which was a pretty good daily pay for a teenager in those days. Of course, if you did this too much, it could also result in dislocated shoulders. That didn't happen to me, but for decades thereafter I did have a small hardly noticeable bump on one of my shoulders which I have always attributed to those double-bag days.

With caddying you remember the very best and the very worst. There was the full gamut in between these extremes, but more tended to worst than best. The best was a man that ended up with me on the first day of his vacation and had such a good game that he asked for me again and again. Although I was never a stellar golfer, in those days I did periodically hit in the low to mid 80s. Moreover, I read up on the subject a lot, so I was able to advise. It only took a round or two before I came to understand my man and what he was capable of doing with certain clubs. I still think back fondly on that single man and his week of appreciation in having me as a caddy. He actually treated me as a person. The worst was the man who threw his clubs at me after bad shots. I only did one round with him, but I gained an understanding of what so many slaves had to endure in years past. If he could have whipped me with impunity, he would have done so. Although there were more minuses than plusses, I do not regret having been a caddy and I am sorry that this opportunity is no longer available for teenagers.

If I was able to go out on a nine-hole round in the early morning, I would be done between 10:30 and 11:00 a.m. That gave me enough time to run down the mountain along Horicon Ave. into Bolton Landing and then through Rogers Park to the town dock. The key was to get there by 11:30 a.m. so as to meet the "Ticonderoga," otherwise called the "Ti" (see p. 28). This was a large tour boat that sailed out of Lake George Village each day. In the morning at 11:30 sharp it would stop at Bolton Landing to drop off or take on passengers. It would continue north into "The Narrows" and then, at 3:30 p.m., it would stop at Bolton Landing once more on its return trip to Lake George Village. The reason for including it in my work endeavors is because I hauled in quite a bit of money from the passengers of this vessel over the years. A horde of young boys like me would jump into the water on the north side of the dock and beg for money each and every summer day. Most passengers would hurl some nickels and dimes at us, but more fun was had when they threw quarters and half dollars, because that stirred up a frenzy of competition among us beggars. I fought many a young man for the big money, and because I had good solid lungs and more than adequate swimming and diving prowess, I had above average success in garnering the treasure.

Once the Ticonderoga had left the dock and the churning water had settled, the scavenging would begin. As the water was at least 20 feet deep, it took some ability to get to the glistening coins. Those few who came with fins and masks were the bane of existence for purists like me. If ever I carried equipment of this sort to the golf course I would have been in no end of trouble. Suffice to say that I usually made a few dollars from the Ti each day so that, when combined with a successful caddying round at the golf course, had the potential of bringing in $10, not a bad haul at all. "Whenever I dive now, my head hurts just above my eyes." That little note from my diary entry indicates that I was flirting with death, which is about par for the course for most of us Baby Boomers. It's true that we had a lot of freedom in growing up, but a consequence of such freedom is one's mortality, and I had both friends and acquaintances that did indeed follow that sad trajectory.

It was in 1968, the summer between my junior and senior year in high school, that I had my first true job—true being that money was taken out for taxes and Social Security. I had applied to work at No-Ro-Wal, an outboard motor rental establishment in Bolton Landing that was owned by the three Lamb Brothers—Norman, Robert and Walter. My close friend, Corky Lamb, had worked there previously and I had volunteered successfully to the point that I thought I could be a viable candidate. Instead, Cork's father Robert, asked me if I would consider being a dock boy at Lamb Bros. Would I ever! Lamb Bros. was a much larger boat rental establishment located next to the public beach. It mostly had Chris-Craft inboard boats, those incredible vessels of the early 20th century that one sees in *Great Gatsby* like movies. Not only would I get to gas and drive those incredible vessels, but I would be working with my pal. There were ups and downs to the job, as with most jobs, but overall, I loved it and continued to be a Lamb Bros. dock boy for three years. The summer of 1970 was the last time I worked at the boat house and was also my last time at Lake George, because thereafter I was preparing for a career in archaeology.

From 1971 on the definition of work as "paid employment" becomes a little tricky. My mentor at Harvard, Dr. Jeffrey P. Brain, accepted my application to work on his survey project in Mississippi for that summer. I was delighted, but it was also explained to me that although I would be expected to work my tail off for two-and-a-half months in the blistering hot sun of Mississippi, I would not be getting a wage. Dr. Brain had come up through the ranks in the Peabody Museum's Lower Mississippi Survey, and he basically ran his projects as apprenticeships. The young men that he took in the field (and they were still all men up until the mid 1970s) would learn by doing. He would work one-on-one with us, and he actually did, but we should not look at what we were doing as employment. It was training, something that other archaeologists were conducting as field schools wherein the students had to pay for the privilege of participation. Dr. Brain didn't believe that any student who worked for him should have to pay to do so, but at the same time he also didn't feel that they should receive pay. "But I tell you what," he said, "at the end of the summer I will give you $500 in scholarship aid." "Sign me up!" I said.

Over the years I have run my own field projects in the same manner. I never wanted to have students counting hours. There were times that we were going to be on a site for extra

hours in order to finish up digging units or clearing the sift-
ing screens. If the crew was looking at watches and calculating
how much time they could sit around in the days ahead, this
wasn't going to work. Moreover, there were days when we had
solid rain and would put in lab hours. Never was I so merci-
less to have students work lab a full eight hours on a rainy day.
Plus, there were evenings during the week set aside as "lab
nights," at which time the students would familiarize themselves with the artifacts and I would work closely with them in
training. I didn't want students considering these as times to
be paid, because seldom was the work done at such times even
necessary for the project. They were assembling the nuts and
bolts for their lives as archaeologists and remuneration was
not to be the principal reason for their participation. If that is
what they wanted, then I did not want them. However, there
was always scholarship aid at the end of the summer, money
that came out of the grants that I received. This was basically
the way I operated on my projects in the 1970s and 1980s. Life
became more complicated in the 1990s, as payroll systems
often couldn't handle the "calling of archaeology," so adjust-
ments were made. Nevertheless, all students were told that if
they were counting hours on my projects, I'll start sending
them bills for my teaching.

The main thing to garner out of the above is that I was not
paid during my college years to do archaeology, at least not in
the field. Back on campus I was employed by the Director of
the Peabody Museum, Prof. Stephen Williams, to be his student assistant during my junior year (1971–72). That was a
paid position, for which I was very grateful. In my senior year
I was Athletic Secretary for Eliot House and that, too, was a
paid position. Each house at Harvard had about 500 students
in it plus or minus 100, so running the athletic program for a
house was a substantial responsibility. I not only had to work

with other athletic secretaries to schedule games, but I had to make sure that players of the various sports actually showed up at them. I am pleased to say that Eliot House won the Straus Cup in 1972–73, which combines and counts all the intramural sports played on campus. I would like to attribute that success to my organizational skills (not to mention my supreme athletic abilities in soccer, basketball, squash and softball), but Eliot House had a habit of winning the Straus Cup just about every year anyway, so the credit goes more to pride of place than any individual organizer's worth. Nevertheless, I got paid for what I did, and every buck helped.

I am a little ashamed that I never actually needed to work for money in my time at Harvard. My family just barely eked out an existence for most of my early years, but by the time I went to college my father owned his own business (Northeastern Scales) and had two employees, three if you consider my mother who was on the payroll for some reason that I never quite understood or investigated. For Harvard, my family must have had enough financial security that I was no longer receiving any scholarship aid beyond my sophomore year (I don't think). Looking back, paying tuition, room, and board must have been a burden for my parents, but somehow they did it. If it was a problem, they never mentioned it to me. Although I did earn some money, I never had to, and it never went into the till.

My mother and father paid fully for my undergraduate education. I wish I had them around now to thank them for building a life for me that was better than theirs; or at least they considered it to be better, and I suppose I do too. With that said, I can still remember driving up to Lake George once, with my Mom at the wheel. I don't know what the stimulus was, but I said something about how great my childhood had been. My mother beamed with pleasure, because she was never really certain how much she meant to me. Sometimes I wish I had been a bit nicer growing up and was more generous in my compliments. I remember in 1982, when I was teaching at Harvard, one of my students at Harvard asked me how old my parents were. I said they were in their late 60s. "Oh, how you must cherish them!" she declared. I was taken aback because I knew I had not cherished them enough and, sadly, never did when they were alive.

In Graduate School at Brown I had a $2,000 loan to help me get through my first semester in the fall of 1973. I went there with neither scholarship aid nor teaching assistantship, so I knew that I was going to have to get a loan for each and every semester as I worked on my M.A and Ph.D degrees. I could no longer expect my parents to foot the bill for my graduate education, but I also knew that if my performance was not of the highest, there was little chance that I would receive the limited funds that were available at Brown at the time. Consequently, I never worked as hard in my life as I did that first semester in order to excel in academics. My reward was the offering of a teaching assistant position for the second semester. The course was Introduction to Cultural Anthropology, which was not exactly my forte. Even so, I managed to stay one step ahead of the students and that got me through that first major experience of having to teach sections. For the next three years of my time in residence at Brown, I had T. A. positions or a librarian position. The latter was set up for me to establish and organize the departmental library, but what it really did was give me time to work on my dissertation.

I left Brown in 1977 with an M.A. in hand (1975), a new bride by my side, and a dissertation that was close to being finished. When Harvard hired me to do fieldwork on Avery Island, my first permanent job as an archaeologist, that ended my "Early Work" era. I received my doctorate in 1979 (I was determined to get all three degrees in the same decade), at which time my Research Assistant position at the Peabody Museum was elevated to Research Associate. I spent a total of 13 years at Harvard in a variety of roles, including Lecturer, Associate Curator of North American Collections, and Assistant Director of the Peabody Museum. I came to the University of Alabama in January of 1991 just as the first bombs were bursting in Baghdad. That may seem an ominous beginning for my time here, but it was not. I was well prepared for three decades (29.5 years actually) of life and work at the good old U of A. There have been both good and bad times, but more good than bad and, most importantly, I have never had to seek other employment along the way. Alabama has treated me well financially, thus enabling a retirement wherein I can read and write with abandon and not have to worry about mowing lawns or shoveling snow.

Reading, Writing, and Arithmetic

"I CANNOT LIVE WITHOUT BOOKS." THE QUOTE IS ATTRIBUTED TO Thomas Jefferson who, late in life, moved to an abode without his library. If I could mess with the master somewhat, I would add the word "my," as "I cannot live without my books." Books have been the essence of my life, but it is curious as to just how this happened. Our home in McKownville, a little community just west of Albany, New York, was a very tiny residence. The cluster of matchbox houses strung along Ayre Drive (ours was No. 8), were all post-war establishments, meant to be "starter homes," or at least that is how people regard them now. Until my father eventually converted the attic into a bedroom, there was only one floor to the residence, and there was hardly enough room for the four people in my family to move about, never mind housing books. The shelving in the living room was filled with knick-knacks and pictures, but only a scattering of anything to read. We really couldn't afford the expense. Once, when my mother left my father home alone with Jennifer and me, he somehow managed to purchase from a traveling salesman a complete set of encyclopedias and a six-volume set of Hemingway novels. My mother was furious, because his inability to say no to a fast-talking stranger probably amounted to a mortgage payment.

The cause of my father's trip to the doghouse is somewhat ironic because my mother was the one to read books, not my father. I actually think that he may have had a fear of them. In any event, he certainly resented anyone reading books when he was in the room. My father was a talker, not a reader, and anyone in earshot was subject to conversation. I should add to this that he was a most knowledgeable man. Because he read the daily newspaper from front to back, he was always up on current events and that alone gave him much to talk about. With the exception of my mother, who effectively ignored him when so desired, no one else was allowed to go into their own private literary world with Dad in the room.

As stated, my mother was an avid reader. She gravitated towards fiction, and fiction alone. She often said she exhausted three libraries in Morecambe (England) where she grew up, and I do believe that to be true. Many a trip I would take with her to the Albany Public Library to get her weekly quota of books. Each stack sat on the end table beside the couch next to her designated seat, to be poured over once domestic tasks were completed. When my mother started a book, she would not let it go until it was finished, even though the enterprise might be killing her. I think the only volume she actually did abandon was *Ulysses*, and I cannot blame her for doing so. I thought about her as I waded through Joyce's masterpiece in later years. I did finish it, but only because every few pages he managed to titillate my senses with some creative wordsmithing. Otherwise I vary somewhat from my mother's strategy. If a book has not caught me at the end of 100 pages, it's toast. There are just too many books out there to read without being bogged down with nonsense.

But let me return to my youth. I have a vivid image of the Albany Pine Hills Library. This old rambling building had bookshelves everywhere, even up and down the stairwell. Just being surrounded by thousands upon thousands of volumes made me feel good. I would curl up into a cozy little vestibule, much like Jane Eyre as a child, and close myself off from the rest of the world. To this little boy, me, to be enveloped by books was largely akin to nirvana. But home was different. If there were books at all, they tended to be of the medical variety, as my mother reckoned herself to be somewhat of a doctor. There were a couple of pictures in one of these books that my sister Jennifer and I scrutinized with great interest, but that's neither here nor there. We did have some books to our name, but not a great range. One set stands out in my mind. Each year we received from relatives in England a new volume of the *Rupert* books. Contained within were exciting stories of Gypsies, Girl Guides (equivalent to our Girl Scouts), imps, and all sorts of animal creatures that shared adventures with Rupert the Bear. These hardbound illustrated books were our treasures, and over the years they have continued to entertain two more generations of offspring.

Picture books, especially comics, were an important part of my early literary career. Denny Richardson, an older friend in my neighborhood, now sadly deceased, was an only child. As often happens with youths that lack siblings, he was "spoiled," or at least that is the way my mother would (and did) characterize him. He had anything and everything he wanted, including a dog and a pool table! But, more to the point, he had a comic book collection that turned me green with envy. I used to go up to the attic of his house, the entire floor of which was his bedroom, and pour through his collection of comics. I always gravitated toward the Archie series. In my mind's eye I can still see the cover of one issue that had a very young Archie donning glasses to ward off the juice from a squirting grapefruit. As Archie and his friends got older, my heart throbbed for Veronica, an absolutely beautiful brunette. Sigh.

I knew I would never be able to have a collection the size of Denny's because my parents just couldn't (or wouldn't, I was convinced at the time) spring for the dime that each comic cost. Consequently, comics came to me only sparingly. Usually I would receive several at special events such as vacations, mostly to keep me busy on long car trips, but at the rate they accumulated, I knew that they would never amount to a library. And then a miracle happened. In a day when children were allowed to venture forth into the woods alone, the only stipulation being to report in for lunch, I came across a stack of dilapidated cardboard boxes. I opened one of them and almost keeled over. There were comics contained within them, dozens if not hundreds of issues, all due to the house cleaning of some heartless mother. Not only were there Archie comics, but there were Bugs Bunny, Porky Pig, Dagwood, Mutt and Jeff, Little Dot, Spooky, Casper, Chip 'n' Dale, Daffy Duck, and on and on. There were even several Superman comics that dated back to the early 1950s if not the 40s, and the prize of them all was the first issue of Richie Rich, the Poor Little Rich Boy. When last I priced it (circa 2000), it was worth $90 in its fair to good condition. If only my parents had taken stock and invested in my incessant plea to purchase comics! As a lad, however, I wasn't much interested in selling my comics, and nor am I now, but it sure is nice to know that they have value to someone beyond myself.

Although I did not realize it at the time, the most important comics in that treasure trove discovered in the woods were the Classic Illustrated series. From these I learned the stories for novels such as *The Count of Monte Cristo, The Last of the Mohicans, Oliver Twist, 20,000 Leagues Under the Sea, Hamlet, Macbeth, Abraham Lincoln,* and *The Crisis.* It was perhaps from the latter two comics that the Civil War era started to stir in my brain. Later in life I read all of the books listed above and, quite naturally, drew greater satisfaction from the writings, but it was the Classic Illustrated comics that started the ball rolling by introducing me to the tales. I would be remiss not to mention one of these "volumes," as it perhaps influenced me more than all of the rest put together. It was called *Picture Stories from the Bible*, the complete Old Testament edition. It was because of this marvelous book, which is 230 pages long, that I learned about Moses battling the Egyptians, David slaying Goliath, Abraham preparing to sacrifice his son, Elijah being fed by the ravens, etc. Each of the stories was absolutely mesmerizing and I knew them like the back of my hand. It goes without saying that in Sunday School I was the absolute master of the Bible, and though I was but a child it certainly affected my ego to have the admiration of teachers. I, like my church mates, stumbled through the real *Old Testament* at a slow pace, but because I knew where the adventures were leading, the reading was easier. I still have this Picture Stories comic book, nicely bound for a future generation of readers of the "CliffsNotes" ilk.

I am afraid I have got too caught up in my youth, as regards my attachment to books, but before leaving the comics, I must make mention of Uncle Scrooge. Whoever was responsible for creating the Uncle Scrooge tales needs an award, perhaps a Pulitzer, because I defy you to find a kid who has read one and not been carried away with excitement. The story that sticks in my mind, the one that actually had an impact on the trajectory of my life is the adventure that Uncle Scrooge, Donald Duck, Huey, Dewey, and Louie had among the Incas. In scaling a mountain to get to one city high above the clouds (obviously based on Machu Picchu), they stumbled upon a lost generation of Incans who still believed the Spaniards were coming to get them. Consequently, they designed a myriad of booby traps to thwart the onslaught of the Duck family. How silly it sounds to relate this story now, but I was hooked on archaeology as a result of this comic book. It is no accident that the first area course that I took in college was on the archaeology of South America, as I had some aspiration at the time of becoming an

Incan archaeologist. That was not to be, because other books and influences came my way, but Machu Picchu still remains on my list of places I want to visit.

At some time in elementary school I was introduced to the "We Were There" series of books. Titles such as *We Were There at the Battle of the Alamo* and *We Were There at the Boston Tea Party* immediately come to mind. These were absolutely wonderful introductions to history, and I do hope that they were faithful to the truth to some extent. The other books that I read, one after another, were biographies of historical figures. I'm sure the series had a title, but for the life of me I cannot remember it. They were small blue books that had the silhouette of the person on the cover of each volume. The one I remember most was about someone named Thomas Jackson. I was tricked by the title, as I thought it was going to be about a President (either Jefferson or Jackson—can't remember which), and I was already well into the book before I figured out it was about a boy who would become a general in this mysterious thing called The Civil War. His life actually did end up fascinating me, as anyone nicknamed "Stonewall" just had to be interesting.

More and more the Civil War era was entering my life and that is probably because of the highly celebrated centennial of the holocaust that tore our nation apart wherein brother fought brother. I was fascinated by why such a strange conflict like this would have come about in the first place. It was about this time that I saw the movie "Gone with the Wind," a most incredible production. Vivian Leigh substituted for Veronica in my burgeoning interests in the opposite sex. When the movie showed at the Madison Theater, also in Pine Hills near the library, my sister and I saw it twice in one day. I think my mother was delighted to have the time to herself. I didn't actually read Margaret Mitchell's famous novel until I was a senior in high school, and when that happened, I almost failed a final exam. I just couldn't put the book down. And now, courtesy of a recent gift from my son Cabot, I own a leather-bound Franklin Library edition of this great volume—more on the Franklin Library books later.

On the subject of the Civil War, it was in the early 1960s, when I was about 10 years old, that I was gifted the "Battle of the Blue and Gray" soldier set. Many an hour I spent managing that set, often with friends, but just as often alone. I would head off to a sandlot near my house, one that had plenty of hills and dales, and set up the soldiers in strategic positions. I preferred the gray, knowing full well that they had a distinct disadvantage. Not only were there far less of them in the box than their blue equivalents, but the Rebel snipers toppled over easier than the Yankees. Whereas the Yankee sniper laid flat, the Rebel one squatted on one knee. It was nearly impossible to flip the blue sniper, even with a well-placed stone, so I suspect that the designer of this game must have been from Ohio. He sure wasn't in favor of the Confederacy coming out on top!

Although I was a good reader as a child, I was not a great one. I wrestled with those horrible colored card boxes that tested reading acumen and was hard-pressed to advance out of a certain color batch—and it wasn't for lack of trying. At one time one of my teachers, although impressed with my determination, saw that I was trying to read far above my capabilities. As I was checking *Gulliver's Travels* out of the library, she warned, "That's too old for you. You best try something easier." Cynic! Philistine! Swiftly I carried my book to the counter and signed it out; with spite I would prove her wrong. A week later I returned it rather sheepishly and with no fanfare whatsoever because it was indeed too advanced for me. I also tried to read *A Tale of Two Cities* at an early age, because what youth was not fascinated by the guillotine? This youth, as it turned out, because I abandoned in a few pages what I learned in later life is truly a magnificent book. I just wasn't quite ready.

I continued to read historical novels in my teenage years, mostly of the adventure type. I especially liked Robert Louis Stevenson, Nordhoff and Hall's *The Bounty Trilogy*, Walter D. Edmunds *(Drums along the Mohawk)*, James Fennimore Cooper's Leatherstocking tales, and anything by Kenneth Roberts *(Northwest Passage, Arundel, Rabble in Arms*, etc.). As a result of growing up in Upstate New York, stories of the French and Indian War and the Revolutionary War had very special meaning to me. These were true events that occurred on my own stomping grounds. I also became enamored with Agatha Christie at an early age. I think the first book that I read of hers was actually a play. I was very active in Albany Civic Theater as a 12 to 14-year-old and, as most of the kid roles were bit parts, I spent a good deal of time by myself in the upstairs' dressing room area waiting to go on. It was a converted fire station and to get to the stage you had to descend a very narrow spiral stair (not all firemen used poles). In addition to doing homework on rehearsal nights, I also explored the reading material that was stored in the dressing room. It was then that I stumbled upon Christie's play, "Ten Little Indians." It began as a book *(And Then There were None)*, which I now own, but the play was just as fascinating to me. I was hooked on Christie from then on, but one of her mysteries plagues me to this day—*The Murder of Roger Akroyd*. What annoys me about it is that all the clues were there, all of them, but as I just hadn't been able to put them together, the ending came to me as quite a shock. "Witness for the Prosecution" is another one of Christie's plays that baffled me when first I saw it as a movie. I ended up producing that play at Harvard's Eliot House when I was a sophomore, and also produced J. M. Barrie's "Peter Pan" as a senior, but as I am drifting once more into other realms of life, let me return to books. Suffice to say that I always encourage my students to read the products of good mystery writers and to think about the clues offered therein. Clues are about all we ever get in archaeology, and far too few of them I might add!

Mark Twain is my idol. *The Adventures of Tom Sawyer* and *Huckleberry Finn* were the writings that captured me as a child, but as I entered college much more of an impact on me were *The Innocents Abroad* and *Life on the Mississippi*. It was perhaps because of the latter book that I ended up in Mississippi as my first archaeological experience. A fieldwork opportunity came my way during my sophomore year in college that played quite well into this interest.

In the first week of my Harvard experience I had plenty of time on my hands. As Freshmen got to Cambridge a week before upperclassmen and the commencement of classes, it was hoped that we would be accustomed to the waters before the flood began. The inertia was killing me though, as I felt like I should be learning something. One night I took the Red Line to the Boston Common and strolled through a historic cemetery (at night!)—that's where I found Sam Adams; the body, not the beer. And at another time I remember wandering around Harvard's Museum of Comparative Zoology. I happened upon a door that had the name Nabokov on it, Vladimir Nabokov. What an unusual name that seemed. From what I could gather, he did research on moths and butterflies, hence the MCZ connection. Not long thereafter I looked up his name at the Lamont Library and discovered he had some other interests as well. His *Lolita* was the first book that I read in college, excepting the Freshman Week book, Robert Heinlein's *Stranger in a Strange Land*. I am not a lover of science fiction and never have been, but I did like Heinlein's book. For the last five decades I have occasionally used the expression "I grok" in paper commentary, thus driving puzzled students to dictionaries to find out who exactly it is that now inhabits DrB's body.

Also on that same trip to Lamont Library during Freshman Week, or maybe a little later, I ended up in the Hs of the fiction section. The first book I pulled out was Thomas Hardy's *Tess of the D'Urbervilles*. Although I found it difficult to read, eventually I did complete it and did like it. It certainly must have left an impression on me because I have continued to read Hardy forever after and believe I have exhausted all the prose that he wrote—the poetry? Heaven forbid! *The Return of the Native* is perhaps my favorite Hardy novel, as my son well knows. When he was a 15-year-old lad he accompanied me, yelling and screaming all the way, along the path behind Hardy's Cottage in Dorset, the location where all the landmarks of this wonderful book played out.

I have always liked to follow in the footsteps of favored fiction authors. My love of novels, especially those that involve travel, began early in life, but was most stimulated by three courses that I took in college. I don't have the exact titles for them, but the first was The Literature of Travel, taught by Robert H. Chapman, which I took during my second semester of college. While most students went on strike protesting the Kent State Massacre in 1970, I myself returned to campus in order to take the final exam and ace the course—for shame. It was during this class that I continued to read Twain and was also introduced to Poe (*The Narrative of Arthur Gordon Pym*), Defoe (*Robinson Crusoe*), Mandeville (*The Travels of...*), Melville (*Typee*), and many others. Edgar Allan Poe was already a hero of sorts for me, as I had read his tales of the macabre as a youth, and also even acted out some of them in one-act plays ("The Tell-Tale Heart"), but *Pym* was a novel, and indeed was a surprise. The second course that impacted me, as regards books, was totally focused on Leo Tolstoy. While I was reading

War and Peace, Anna Karenina, Resurrection, The Cossacks, and dozens of Tolstoy stories, my roommate (Henry Moreta) was taking the companion course on Fyodor Dostoevsky. As a result of these courses and the conversations that went on with Henry into the late hours of many evenings, I have always had a fondness for Russian Literature.

The third course in college that affected my life with books was British Literature of the 19th century. It was at this time that I read Jane Austen, the Bronte sisters, Thackeray, Dickens, Galsworthy and many others. *Wuthering Heights* had an effect on me like no other book ever has. Many years later, I ventured to Top Withens near Halifax, supposedly the stimulus for Emily's one and only novel. This time, with nephew Trevor Hughes as companion, we made the long trek to these desolate ruins on the moors. As I was musing upon the surroundings that so inspired Emily, I noticed in the distance a young woman who was jogging along the path in our direction. With long black hair flowing behind her much like a mane, she brought to mind an episode of the novel, and stimulated me to address her as she passed. "Cathy?" She turned, laughed, and without hesitation responded, "And are you my Heathcliffe?" The one very nice attribute of this British literature course was that the students were required to maintain a journal of their readings for at least 10 of the novels. Imagine, 10! If I were to have assigned that many books in one of the college classes that I myself taught, I would be drummed out of the university! The times, they have indeed changed.

So much for "Reading." As regards "Writing," the second subject of this essay, I have always maintained a book journal of sorts. Early on in my elementary school years I was given a fairly thick (or so it seemed at the time) journal to record the books that I read. There were six or seven slots per page in the booklet, leaving ample space to record my thoughts. The enlightened teacher who instituted this assignment only expected us to maintain the journal for the year, but I continued to enter book titles, summaries, and critiques for every volume I read throughout my teen years. I suppose that fledgling literary volume is somewhere in my holdings, or perhaps in my sister's cottage in Maine, but I have not seen it for decades so cannot be sure that it has survived the ravages of time. I doubt that it would have been thrown away, because my mother always admired that I wrote in it so diligently. She said that she wished she too had kept such a record of all the books she had ever read, which in and of itself was one of the nicest compliments I have ever received.

I first discovered that I had at least a capacity for writing at the end of my freshman year in college. The Literature of Travel course referred to above required a major term paper and I opted to write mine on a personal travel narrative. In the summer of 1969, several months before heading off to Harvard, my good friend Corky Lamb and I and two girls whose reputations are secure by my not giving their names did a full-day trip in my boat. We traveled from Bolton Landing on the west shore of Lake George to the northern limits of this great body of water, just south of Ticonderoga. What incredible sights we saw en route, many of which I could describe with the authority of direct observation. Some important spots that had historical significance were for some reason missed by us, but I rectified the matter by including second-hand descriptions of them in the paper that I turned in. What a sad admission to make, but I attribute it to the vagaries of youth. Despite a smattering of falsity in the narrative, purely the product of imagination, the paper itself exuded praise from my professor and received an A grade as a result. Perhaps I was a writer?

I could not be a writer. I was a Mathematics major in college. My guidance counselor in high school had a long talk with me in my junior year. I expressed an interest in history and said that I would like to be an archaeologist. "But your best courses are math," he said. "You have scored in the high 90s in geometry, algebra, trigonometry, and you'll be taking college-level calculus in your senior year. Ian, you need to be doing something in the mathematics field." I think I said something very profound like, "Okay. What?" "You need to be an engineer," he said, to which I acquiesced. My parents were deliriously happy by my decision. I applied to Union College, Clarkson, and Cornell in New York State and got into all three, with full State Regent Scholarships at each. Had I gone to any of these fine institutions I would be a civil engineer today, but I went to Harvard instead and registered at the end of my freshman year as a Mathematics major.

I did well in my math courses at Harvard, but apparently had not chosen wisely. Before registering for sophomore year, I met with my math advisor who was a graduate teaching assistant. I said something to the effect that I wanted to write an Honors Thesis in my senior year. "You're too far behind," he said. "If you were going to write a thesis you should have been taking such and such math courses in your freshman year." The only lasting memory from my discussion with him was that at the ripe old age of 18 I could not master my field to the level of writing an Honors Thesis. I was just too far behind and, moreover, I lacked the skills. That was bad enough, but on top of that, I was absolutely bored. I could do basic calculus well because I enjoyed solving puzzles, but that enjoyment went out the window by my sophomore year when the next level of calculus became theoretical. I even started to question whether I should be in college at all.

Fortunately, at some time during my freshman year I read James Michener's *The Source*. It is about a Near Eastern tell and an archaeologist. The dig starts at the top and goes down to the bottom, to the spring, to the source. Once the digging ends, the second half of the book takes off, with tales of what really happened on each occupation level. As a result of reading *The Source*, I started to reevaluate the direction of my life. I spent the summer of 1970 on Lake George, one last gasp at being a kid. I can still remember lying in the bilge of a boat late one night, somewhat inebriated, looking up at the sky, and having an epiphany moment. I signed up for the introductory archaeology course in the fall and switched majors from Mathematics to Anthropology in the second semester of sophomore year. My reading and writing from then on changed markedly. Archaeology hovers between the social sciences and the humanities and that, to me, is a good thing.

Over the years I have exhausted many authors and they have also both exhausted and excited me. The project that has kept me busiest these past half dozen years is reading each and every one of the Franklin Library Classic series, the world's greatest books. I do so one at a time, and in alphabetical order. If I didn't do it this way, I would have ended up reading all the books that I wanted to read first, thus leaving all the poetry to the end, and with a latent wish that the Grim Reaper would strike me dead before concluding the project. Proceeding alphabetically has forced me to consume books in a specific order and, as a result, I have ventured deeply into writings that I suspected were not going to be my cup of tea, and yet often turned out to be a very fine brew—and yes, that does include poetry.

A problem that I am hesitant to relate is that I have a marked tendency to forget what I have read. I am now on Z in my Franklin Library Project (Émile Zola's *Nana*), but for the life of me I cannot list the last five books I have read.[6] Forget-

---

6 I have actually completed the project now and am busily typing up the hand-written journals.

ting what I read is an admitted weakness, but my strength, such as it is, is that I review and critique as I read, and when I do want to remember the classics, or any book for that matter, I have both the Franklin Library Project journals (there are six of them) and my diaries to turn back to. And somewhere back in the bowels of that cottage in Maine are the book reviews from my childhood years, all carefully listed and described.

I shall end this discourse on reading, writing and arithmetic with a note about cataloguing, surely an endeavor of the mathematical mind. Ever since my first year in graduate school I have catalogued all books that have entered my library. I have multiple 3x5 card catalogue drawers that contain the title of every single book that I own, or that I have owned, as many have been given away to students or others at various times. Once I make up a card, my name is applied to the title page of the book. I have done this simply so that I know that the book has been entered into my library. Each time I put my name in a book I know that it devalues the volume—horrors upon horrors—but as I have no attention of actually selling any of this collection during my lifetime, any loss that is incurred by having my signature displayed

Ian W. Brown

is suffered solely by inheritors, and if they deign to complain to me now, then I'll know exactly where their sentiments lie. The value of these books inevitably decreases anyway because I tend to write notes in them. I always use graphite, never ink, and more often than not only a small dot, a check, or an asterisk are entered as marginalia. A blank page or two, or three (Damn Boswell and his *Life of Johnson!*) at the back of the book contain more detailed notes, all good fodder for if and when I end up writing reviews of said books or as grist for new books that I fashion.

I hated the onset of the digital age because almost over-night those thousands of cards stored in file cabinets had become obsolete. I knew very early on that someday it would be advantageous to enter these cards on to the computer, in-cluding of course the detailed notes that I have on the back of them. Sometime in 1989, when I was curating the Hall of the North American Indian exhibition at Harvard's Peabody Museum, I was rapidly approaching a deadline to create cap-tions for the cases. I not only had to write detailed labels for hundreds of objects, but also required were group labels and introductory panels. I was procrastinating, and deep down I knew that if I didn't start soon Rick Riccio, the exhibit de-signer, would not be able to have them ready for our sched-uled opening in April of 1990. I can still remember sitting at my desk on the second floor of the Peabody overlooking the Tozzer Library courtyard. It was a crystal-clear day without a cloud in sight. My mind started to wander on such a nice sun-ny day, especially as the window was open a crack and the air was so refreshing. I deemed it a perfect day to start converting my card catalogue to a digital format. Thus, I pulled out the first drawer, selected the first card, and typed the book title into my computer. A bolt of lightning, out of the blue, struck within the courtyard. I did not jump. I did not flinch. All I did was pick up the card, place it back in its tray, and proceeded to write the first caption for the exhibition that has turned out to be the most lasting achievement of my career. The Hall of the North American Indian exhibition that I curated, called "Change and Continuity in Native American Lifeways," is but a book on the wall, carefully curated and imprinted by a strike from above that provided me with a definite and most poi-gnant message, gratefully received.

Confessions of a Book Buyer

MY HOME AND OFFICE ARE FILLED WITH BOOKS, THOUSANDS OF THEM in fact. I have been collecting volumes on a myriad of subjects for half a century, with accumulation having increased in rapidity during my Graduate School years at Brown University in the mid 1970s. As stated in the previous essay, all of my books are catalogued and all are arranged alphabetically by subjects. I would also like to say that all my books have been read, but that would be a bold-faced lie. Few have been read, but many have been "read-at" and just about all are known to me. Whether from cataloguing, shifting them around, dusting shelves, or simply searching for a misplaced volume, I do know my library. If a topic is mentioned, or for some reason I desire information, I know where in my vast library to go to be illuminated. Admittedly, Google has cut down on some of this book-oriented research of late, but the archaeologist in me realizes that Google will not be around forever, and that Wikipedia's future is very much tied to its funding. Books will not last either, so says Ray Bradbury, but they are at least hard tangible objects that I can hold in my hands. And even when they sit there unread, their very existence in my personal library offers a security of knowledge, akin to a play in the round with me at center. To stretch the metaphor, my library is there for the drinking, if only I have a willingness to imbibe. There is of course a stratification to my library. Paperbacks, even of the non-fiction ilk, do not have the same allure to me as hardback books, and nothing compares with those leather-bound gilt-edged tomes of the Franklin Library for giving me a sense of scholarship, all in addition to the warmth and comfort of my surroundings.

So, how did this all come about? In the previous chapter I have written about the role books have played in my life, which is not the intent of this particular essay. Suffice to say that although I have always liked to read, the actual desire to acquire books did not occur until my post teenage years. That interest began when I started to think of myself as an academic, a hopeful aspiration to be sure. With limited budget, however, a failing which seemed to go on forever, or at least until children were out of the home and safely engaged in their own life endeavors, I always had to be careful as to how much I spent on books on any specific occasion. In short, I was always looking for bargains, and still am for that matter.

Thank the Lord for the Tozzer Book Sale! Every year when I was in college and for many years thereafter the Peabody Museum's Tozzer Library[7] would have a massive annual sale. It seems strange for a university library that is devoted to research and teaching to have a sale of this scale, but the books that were sold at this event were all duplicates. As Harvard Anthropology faculty or alumni retired, many of them donated their books to the Tozzer Library with the understanding that they would be sold to students. The announcement for this annual event was low key, basically limited to current Harvard graduates and undergraduates and museum personnel. However, the doors were open to all at such times and I would often come up from Brown University in my Graduate years with a bevy of very grateful students of my cohort, much

---

7 This library is named after Alfred Marston Tozzer, Harvard's great Mayan archaeologist and a professor to generations of Mesoamerican scholars. It was once the library of the Peabody Museum of Archaeology and Ethnology, but now falls within the ownership and management of the Harvard University Library system. It still is closely tied to Peabody faculty and staff though, or at least I think that is so.

to the chagrin of Harvard students, many of whom were still friends (at least I think they were)—but how dare I bring intruders into the mix!

The books at the Tozzer sale were priced so low it defied imagination. Paper-bound monographs went for a couple of dollars and hardbacks were only $5, if that. Moreover, when one opened the pages of these offerings, the signatures of many 20th-century Anthropologists greeted the eye. To be able to own copies that once had graced the libraries of the founders of my field was simply unbelievable. Many of these books remain in my library today as treasured items, but as I am now halfway through the 70th year of my life, I am beginning to wonder what will become of them? Will others share the thrill of owning works that belonged to the heroes of the past, and which often have marginalia made by them within, or will these books end up in a dumpster or recycling bin? I wake up nights worrying about such things.

My library holdings grew during Graduate School, enough for me to realize that moving to different abodes was becoming a bit of a problem. When I went to college in 1969, a single carload of personal belongings was all that was necessary to set up my dorm in Cambridge, and for my move to Providence in 1973 two carloads were more than sufficient for the task. In the fall of 1977, following our marriage, Easty and I moved to Avery Island in Louisiana. Just about everything we owned was shipped there, including my books, and it was then that problems started to enfold. It can be stated quite simply—books are heavy and moving them is costly. This problem has not only remained throughout my life, but it has magnified exponentially, almost beyond belief. "Never again!" I said in our 2018 move from Derby Downs Drive to our Guildswood home in Tuscaloosa's historic district, and though I said this in the context of house purchasing, the stimulus for the outburst was directly related to carting back and forth hundreds of boxes of books between homes. The insult to my injury was compounded by the simultaneous shifting of an equivalent number of books from office to office.[8]

When we left Avery Island in 1979, we rented the largest U-Haul truck they had available to move our belongings to Watertown so as to assume my new position at the Peabody Museum.[9] Furniture took up most of the space in that enormous vehicle, but books far outweighed everything else contained within. Twelve years later, when we moved to Alabama, a large moving van was required to move our household across the country and books were by far the bulk of the load. The estimates made by the movers were off by 50%, a conundrum they discovered when they weighed in at Tuscaloosa. I had warned them repeatedly, "You know books are heavy," but they did not listen. Were it not for the good graces of my Dean, who paid for our move south, I believe I would still be in debtor's prison, because the movers were insistent that an estimate was just an estimate.

As I have now laid the groundwork for how books own me, let me reverse gears and look at how that accumulation occurred over time. Easty and I did a lot more book buying in the 1980s. Trips to Maine almost always entailed us taking U.S.

---

8 At the same time that we were moving into the historic district, I was moving out of the Chair's office in the University of Alabama's Anthropology Department, following a stint of five years duration. All of the books in that facility were returned to the GCS (Gulf Coast Survey) offices and lab in the Mary Harmon Bryant Building where they had been previously housed. The expression, "I pick things up. I put things down," is commonly used by me to describe both house and work endeavors when related to books.

9 With doctorate now in hand (a June graduation), I was promoted from Research Assistant to Research Associate with the Peabody Museum's Lower Mississippi Survey and headed north to analyze collections and write reports. Little did I realize at the time that my employment at Harvard would last another decade or so, more than ample time for increasing the breadth and scope of a personal library.

Rt. 1, "the Slow Road" that paralleled the coast, largely because there were innumerable used bookstores along its borders. More often than not our travel time to Port Clyde to visit with my mother and father took twice the expected time. Things changed considerably in 1983, when Avery was born, because no longer could we dally so long looking for books. Once we got to Port Clyde and could be free of baby (later toddler and baby) for a few hours, we often sought out the many bookstores in and around Camden. Getting good books cheaply was the objective because we always seemed to be on a very limited budget. We did have our favorite places, but we soon learned that whether or not they remained our favorites depended on the turnover of each establishment. What I mean by this is that when I would first go into a used bookstore it was always like Xmas. Up and down the aisles I would go. I inevitably started with history and anthropology, especially archaeology, but if there was time, I would check out multiple topics. With paperbacks, if they were priced over $10 I would generally move on. For hardbacks the turning point for me usually was $20. And I still feel the same way. Even though I can now afford to pay more, I don't feel like I am getting a good deal with used books if costs exceed these amounts. Rare books are another matter. For those volumes I am willing to pay more if I really want the books and deem the costs justifiable.

After a visit or two, those places that at first seemed like Xmas in July often changed for me; or rather, my attitude changed simply because I found the places to be stagnant. What I mean by this is that if I continued to see the exact same books on the same crowded shelves, I knew there was not much of a turnover to the place. And if the prices remained the same, that meant to me there was no real effort to move things along. The sellers basically were content with hitting up "newbies" but cared little for "returners." Used bookstores that I would eventually come to avoid were characterized by piles of books in awkward places, limited chairs that always had books piled on them, and a scowling proprietor who looked askance at anyone coming through the door bearing a box of books for sale, or even if they just wanted to leave them. It is understandable why that would be the case if the bookstore was small and if a method had not been developed for moving books in and out. Money can be made by passing travelers of course, but the local clientele, the repeat customers, would stop coming if they always knew what to expect. There just was no incentive for them to return.

I could go on and on but will spare the reader. Between library book sales, bargains sought and gained at numerous used bookstores around the country, membership in the History Book Club and the Folio Society, and now a loyal client at my wife's store, Ernest & Hadley Booksellers, my personal library has grown to a point of personal satisfaction. By my estimate, I would at least need three more lifetimes to read (never mind understand) all of the books in my holdings, but even with this recognition, I continue to buy books. A friend of the family once told my wife, "You know, your husband has a problem." I think she was suggesting a book hoarding issue, which may be true, but as her critique could apply to a variety of ills, I did not pursue the matter.

Academia

(I NEVER PLANNED TO BE A COLLEGE PROFESSOR)

DOCTORS AND MINISTERS HAVE CALLINGS. I NEVER HAVE BEEN interested in such trades, so I did not have a calling. If anything, I had a "telling." As mentioned previously, my high school guidance counselor met with me at the end of my junior year, looked over my grades, and said "You're best in math. What do you think about being a civil engineer?" "Not much," I thought, as I was far more interested in history. But he knew best, so I said okay and ended up applying to various colleges that focused on engineering, including Clarkson, Union, and Cornell, all solid schools that would accept my New York State Regents Scholarship. I got into all of the engineering colleges, which was nice, but I also got accepted into Harvard, which was even nicer. Harvard College was not so specialized as to have a focus on engineering for undergraduates, but what they do have is a Mathematics major, so that is what I signed up for at the end of my freshman year.

Midway through my sophomore year, however, I discovered that I wanted to be an archaeologist, a vocation that had haunted me (in a good way) since I was about seven years old when I was taken on a dig for a day. I discovered in college (eventually) that archaeology was listed under anthropology, so that is what I ended up majoring in. I had no idea at the time what an anthropologist was, but I really didn't have a choice—"American archaeology is anthropology or it is nothing."[10] Each summer following my sophomore year I went on a dig, which was heaven on earth. Imagine, being able to have paid summer vacations for every year of your life and rationalize it as work. But how did one get such jobs?

When I was finishing college in 1973 there was no such thing as contract archaeology. Cultural resource management, wherein Uncle Sam requires 5% of projects using federal money to go to CRM (read archaeology) was still a few years in the future. If I wanted to continue having those paid summer vacations, I needed to get some more schooling under my belt. That really meant an M.A. or Ph.D., with the more advanced degree providing me more options. In 1973 there were just three avenues for those trained in archaeology: academia, museums (the bigger ones), or government work (National Park Service for example). The professors at Brown University, where I did my graduate training, pushed for academia. Their basic philosophy was, "Look at me. I'm a college professor. Don't you want to be one too?" I guess I did, but I don't really know why. Being a tenure-track professor would enable me to do research, which was great, but it would also require teaching, and I wasn't sure I was prepared for that, or would even like it.

The only inkling I had that teaching might be something that wouldn't be totally terrible for me occurred in my senior year of high school. The "fast class" (I'm not sure that's what they called it, but you get the idea) were given the opportunity of being teachers for a day. My good friend Bob MacDowell and I signed up for it. I chose an American history class and prepared by reading the week's assignments and then did a little extra prepping on some material that the students had not read. I ended up teaching a couple of classes during the day,

---

10 An oft-cited quote from Gordon R. Willey and Philip Phillips, *Method and Theory in American Archaeology* (Chicago: University of Chicago Press, 1958), 2.

and at the end of the afternoon met with a teacher who had sat in on them. He said I did well overall, but felt I was a little too relaxed (I sat on the desk!), and all I did was pose questions to the students. A little more lecturing was in order. "And oh, by the way, you and Bob spent too much time in the Teachers' Lounge playing ping pong." Why of course we did. There have to be some perks for teaching after all. My only hope is that this critic did not get tenure.

In the second semester of my first year in graduate school I was assigned to be a Teaching Assistant to Introduction to Cultural Anthropology, which was taught by Tom Kiefer that term and by George Hicks in the next. Hicks was very much a task master, which was fine, but he didn't allow a great deal of flexibility for the T.A.s. I remember mentioning that I was giving the students of my section a session on some topic or another, to which he reacted quite negatively. "That's not what the other T.A.s are doing, and it would be unfair to expect your students to know that." I scratched my head on that one. This teaching business is pretty complex. I can't be relaxed, I can't ask questions of them, and I can't address topics outside the usual and expect them to know more. I wasn't sure I was interested in teaching if that's what was involved, but in Grad School if you wanted funding that's what you did.

Probably the most exciting course for me, and the one that turned me around, was Jim Deetz's (my advisor) course on material culture. In the last year I was at Brown I served as head T.A. for that course, which resulted in his monumental book, *In Small Things Forgotten: An Archaeology of Early American Life*.[11] Jim was everything I admired in a professor. He was totally himself before an audience of 200, paced back and forth thinking as he walked, informed and joked, engaged us with questions, spoke off his slides (never from notes), and abso-

---

11 New York: Doubleday, 1977.

lutely mesmerized us. One fellow T.A. sitting next to me, who became a well-known professor in her own right, looked at me in a daze during one of Jim's lectures. "What's the matter?" I asked her. "I just saw Jim's aura." That was a bit much for me, but it did show me that there might be something to this teaching thing.

1976 came and went. I was done with my dissertation fieldwork and was interested in marrying this very fine woman named Nancy Lambert[12] who I had met on a dig two years previously. If I wanted to make things work, however, I had to have a job. Unfortunately, there weren't many out there in 1976 without having a Ph.D. in hand. I applied to be the State Historical Archaeologist of South Dakota and two weeks later without having been interviewed I got a letter saying that the job was mine and when can I get out there? As I had done this on a whim and as my wife-to-be was not quite enamored with the prospect of honeymooning in South Dakota, I had to tell them that I was still working on my dissertation so must turn down their kind offer. Meanwhile, I applied to South Carolina and to Tulane for tenure-track positions. Lo and behold, I got interviews at both, which was not really what I was expecting as I was in the midst of writing. But what I didn't get from either South Carolina or Tulane were actual job offers. It's very hard being a runner-up, especially when you really do want to get married and settle down.

What did come my way in the summer of 1977 was an offer from Harvard. Steve Williams, who was Director of the Peabody Museum and had been one of my professors there asked me, "How do you know Lanier Simmons?" That was a curious story. Lanier was the wife of Ned Simmons, Vice President

---

12 The reader should note that Nancy Lambert, Nancy Lambert-Brown, and Easty Lambert-Brown are all the same person, but at different times. Nancy became Easty when she turned 60 and remains so today.

of McIlhenny Company, makers of Tabasco Sauce. She also was on the Visiting Committee for the Peabody Museum because of her interests in archaeology and museums, which is how she knew Steve. Lanier was on the Louisiana Antiquities Commission as well, which just happened to be meeting in Baton Rouge when I was returning from my Tulane interview and was staying at Bill Haag's house. Bill was a Professor of Anthropology at LSU and also Louisiana's first State Archaeologist. Lanier and I talked briefly, but certainly not enough for me to have made much of an impression on her. I suspect that Bill must have said something positive on my behalf; something like, "Give the man a job. He's eating me out of house and home!" Steve said that the McIlhennys (Walter and Jack) were wanting to have more archaeological work done on Avery Island and they put Lanier and Ned in charge of making it happen. She came to Steve and said, "We want Ian Brown."

God bless Lanier, Avery Island, and all things Tabasco, as they provided the funding for my job for the next two years, serving first as a Research Assistant for the Peabody Museum's Lower Mississippi Survey and then, once I got my doctorate, as a Research Associate. In the fall of 1979 Easty and I moved to Cambridge to spend the next year writing up the results of my Avery Island work. Steve and Jeff (Brain, my mentor at Harvard in my undergraduate years) encouraged me to write grants so as to help cover my salary. That led to NEH and National Geographic sponsored projects in the Natchez, Mississippi region, so I was able to stay on at the Peabody. Clearly, I was heading for a life as a museum archaeologist.

Steve steered me in a different direction when he asked if I might also like to do a bit of teaching ?He had good relations with the folk in Harvard's Freshman Seminar Program and thought he could get me signed on if I was interested. Without blinking an eye, I said yes, and so became a Lecturer in the

Department of Anthropology. The first course I ever taught as Instructor of Record was on North American Indian ethnohistory. There were only five freshmen in the class I think and all but one of them ended up majoring in Anthropology. This pleased me and apparently pleased some others because I was then assigned to Gen. Ed. 152, the long-running Indians course that attracted many students, mostly because it fulfilled a requirement I suspect. There were no student assessments at that time, of course, but there was a rap sheet of short complaints or praises that college students circulated, and my Gen. Ed. course received many accolades. I was very grateful.

My teaching load at Harvard remained but one a year, as I assumed more and more museum duties (Associate Curator of North American Collections and later Assistant Director of the Peabody Museum). Although I could not keep teaching in the "Day School" after seven years, which was a Harvard ruling at the time, I kept my fingers in the pie by teaching a course in the Extension School each semester. The opportunity to both design and implement the Certificate in Museum Studies Program in the Extension School (which turned 30 in 2018 and is now an M.A. program) was another opportunity that came my way. For the first few years of its existence I taught all of the introductory courses and, simultaneously, served as its Internship Coordinator in addition to my museum duties. All of this came to an end when the permanent exhibition that I developed in the North American Indian Hall was completed in the spring of 1990. Any hope of staying on with an endowed curatorship was dashed when the economy of Boston, the Northeast, and the nation overall collapsed in 1990. Thus, after a dozen years with Harvard, I found myself once again on the job market. I had two very young kids and a hefty mortgage on a recently purchased house, so I was game for anything that came with a paycheck.

Three jobs turned out to be viable options. The Director-ship of the Anthropology Department at the Denver Museum of Natural History was actually offered to me. I would have had quite a large staff and lots of administrative duties, but there was no teaching involved. Also in the mix was Head of Inter-pretations at the Florida Museum of Natural History. There was no teaching for that gig either, but I would come in as a tenured faculty member associated with their Anthropology Department. The University of Alabama was also a possibility, but a longshot. Jim Knight, who I knew somewhat but not well, floated the idea of hiring this guy from Harvard who had a lot of museum and archaeological experience. Doug Jones, Direc-tor of the Alabama Museum of Natural History, had been want-ing an archaeologist on his museum staff for quite some time, especially one who had an interest in the Gulf Coast, which I did. Jim Yarbrough, Dean of the College of A&S at the time, liked the Harvard connection and liked even better that he would only have to pay half my salary. Dick Diehl, Chair of the Anthropology Department, would get an absolute freebie so, as long as I wasn't a jerk, he was quite happy with the prospect.

To me Alabama was the dream position, precisely be-cause I would have a teaching role, one course a semester. But then the bad news came—for the job to materialize it had to be advertised. Why, the audacity of it all! That meant others would be applying.[13] Moreover, I would have to turn down the Denver position without actually having a job in hand. And if the Florida position materialized, I would be forced to take it because the salary would have been almost twice what Ala-bama was willing to pay me. Florida ended up stalling their

---

13 A highly competent archaeologist (and also a friend) who shall go unnamed, actually did apply. Jim, also a good friend of ____ said, "You know ____, that job's for Ian." "Yes, I know," he said, "but he could die before being hired." Now that's what I call a practical man!

position for a year because of the bad economy, so I went ahead and turned down Denver and waited to hear from Alabama. In the meantime, David Pilbeam, the new Director of the Peabody Museum asked me to stay on at the Peabody in order to deal with this thing called NAGPRA, which had just come to his attention.[14] All of a sudden, I had a job again. I thanked him, said I would stay on for the semester, but then I was going south.

In the end the stars aligned. I came to Alabama in January of 1991 as an Associate Professor, with split responsibilities between museum and college. Two years later I was tenured and promoted to Full Professor and in 1997 I came over to the college full time as a result of what I refer to "as that time of unpleasantness" at the museum. Ever since, I have retained my honorary curatorial role with the museum, as well as my offices and lab in the Mary Harmon Bryant building, and have been very grateful for the continued connection.

All in all, as I look back at my career, what a strange route I have taken in academia. The last three decades at the University of Alabama have gone by quickly, far faster than my first dozen years at Harvard when life was young and so was I. Although there have been both ups and downs at Alabama, the ups were far more satisfying than the downs were depressing. No one ever looks back on a career in academia and says, "Gee, I wish I could have had more committee assignments." I have had many of the latter in my time at Alabama and have had more than enough administrative assignments, but the things I remember most are the students that I have advised and the classes I have taught, especially the seminars. De-

---

14 The Native American Graves Protection and Repatriation Act was enacted in November of 1990. This act affected any and all museums and their institutions (like Harvard itself) that ever received or wished to receive federal money. In short, I was still needed at the Peabody Museum.

spite never having had a plan to teach, I am very grateful for that one opportunity I had in high school that permitted me to test the waters. I still don't agree with the critic that said I was far too relaxed and asked too many questions, because that has basically been my mode of operation throughout my career. I'm no Socrates, to be sure, and have acquired no taste for hemlock, but I do share some of his philosophy.

Games and Sports

(A PREPARATION FOR LIFE)

"How do we get kids to read?" This was a question my wife asked of me. As both a publisher and a bookseller, she feels she is not doing her duty to children of middle age. "Between eight and 15 they don't come into the bookstore." I commiserated but told her the same thing I tell historical society folk whenever I give talks at chapter meetings on the subject of cemeteries, "Just wait for them to get older." My argument is that between ages eight and 15 most minds are focused on games and sports; and once puberty starts, there are other distractions. Books just aren't a priority in those fledging years. Let's put sex to the side for a moment and focus on those other two pastimes of youth—sports and games, as these are the things that introduce children to life. Sitting in the bleachers at a Little League baseball game is a lesson in life. All that is good and bad in adults come forth at such venues, and kids "profit" from the experiences. Whereas we, as adults, might look at childhood games and sports as youth ill-spent, they truly are "the work" of a child because what they learn from participating in such endeavors really does prepare them for life. The Duke of Wellington said it best. While watching a cricket match on the grounds of Eton College, he was overheard to say, "The battle of Waterloo was won here." A certain amount of reading is good and important for every child, but I can testify for myself that of games, sports, and books, the latter really does rank third. And for the good of society, let's exclude any issues of intimacy from this particular essay!

As with books and movies, I have no idea what was the first game I ever played or when I may have kicked a ball or caught one in my hand. Much like a kitten or a puppy, I suspect I reacted to whatever my parents threw my way. "Peek-a-boo" always stimulated a reaction, as did praying hands: "Here is the church. Here is the steeple. Open the doors and see all the people." The wiggling of fingers must have aroused all sorts of laughter in me as a babe, and, most importantly, it all came back to me when my daughter Avery was born. She, too, delighted over this mindless game that lasted for as long as she wished it to, because that's what Moms and Dads do.

I suspect that games came before sports in my maturing process. When I was a child there was no preschool or day care. Until the age of five I was under the jurisdiction of my mother. My world consisted of my house and my yard. My friends were the children of immediate neighbors and I was basically told, "These are your friends. Now blow out the candles." I was fortunate because Janet Hiller, who lived in the house next to mine, was my best friend for the first six or seven years of my existence and though we drifted during our teen years we still remain good friends today, for which I am most grateful. Although I do not remember the games we played as children, whether inside or out, the main point is that gaming was the prime mechanism in social development. There needs to be others involved in one's space to develop as a social being, and that is best served when temperaments mesh. There is no profit in playing games wherein the end result is marred by pain and frustration. Losing is sad enough for a child who invests so much energy in an activity, so much heart and soul, but one can handle it if the victor is a good winner. There is nothing worse than a person who exhibits glee at the expense of another. One inevitably feels happiness inside, but to show it at the expense of others is an error of the first order, a lesson of gaming that all children experience, and many adults too.

The main person who taught me the philosophy of gaming, meaning the etiquette involved, was my Uncle Bernard, to the rest of the world known solely as Bernard Dixon. Never did I refer to him without using the appellation "uncle," however, because that term of endearment meant the world to me. Uncle Bernard was not only a kindly relative, but he was the elder, the teacher, the mentor. Moreover, he delighted in children and had the patience of Job. Whenever I (and still referring to the first decade of my life) wanted to play a game, Uncle Bernard was always at my disposal. There are two games in particular that I remember vying with him—chess and hockey. When I say hockey, I'm not talking of the outdoor sort but, rather, a platform filled with metal men who spun in circles swinging at a marble that belted back and forth at lightning speed. One hand of the player would stay permanently fixed on the goalie while the other moved from defense to offense with both dexterity and agility. I was the master of that game and could beat any and all of my friends, but Uncle Bernard was inevitably the victor whenever I played him. He never laughed, he never gloated, but he always asked kindly if I wanted to play again, which of course I did. He never let me win, which must sound heartless to those who follow the writings of Dr. Spock or other parental authorities of the day, but the value to me in my education as a social being is that when I did win I knew I deserved it on my own merits, not through the largesse of others. Once someone knows that a game has been thrown, it loses all its meaning.

The same can be said of chess. Beyond moving the pieces, I don't remember Uncle Bernard ever teaching me strategy. I just watched what he did and with each incidence of defeat a lesson was imprinted on my brain. No child realizes this is happening of course and had he ever laughed or even so much as smiled, the game would have been over. I would have learned a lesson of bullying, which is one of the horrors of growing up, or even of adulthood for that matter. Those who bully learn that art from other bullies, of that I am convinced. I do understand and appreciate the important role of genetics in one's make up but am a firm believer that bullying itself is acquired by personal experience early in life. Because Uncle Bernard never allowed me to win in chess by making stupid moves, in those few occasions when I said, "Checkmate," I knew that it was my skill that won the day and that meant something.

My daughter Avery was never interested in chess, but Cabot was, and he endured the same routine that was taught me. He could beat all his friends in chess, but he could never conquer me. Let me correct that statement. When Cabot was 15 years old, he and I traveled throughout southern England together. It was a true bonding experience because had we been at home at this time in his life, he would not have been at all interested in hanging out with his Dad. At one bed and breakfast that we stayed at in our two-week tour, there was a chess board in the public area. I was doing my usual reading or writing, and Cabot quite clearly was bored out of his mind. He asked me if I wanted to play chess and I said, "Sure." And then an amazing thing happened. For the next hour or so I transitioned from what had been a most tranquil, joyous state to a nervous, twittering fool, absolutely lathered in sweat. At first, I thought it merely an aberration that he had made a good move. I had been on the defensive with his moves previously but always, with patience, I could find the chink in his armor. This time not only did his armor hold, but the knight in shining armor, the brazen bishop, and the rueful rook were having their way with me. The worst part was that for every five minutes that I twisted in my seat, seeping steam from my noggin, he would dither around and then take but seconds to do a countermove. When all was over and done, and with the word "Checkmate" resounding in my ears, I stood up and shook his hand. "Well played my son," I said, "Would you like to play again." Cabot took no evident joy in his victory, and I don't even remember him smiling, but I do remember as if it was yesterday his loaded response, "No, I really don't feel like it." And, much to my chagrin, he did not feel like it for another 10 years, which was the next time that he and I traveled to England together. Once again, he came across a chess board and asked if I wanted to play. "Sure," I said, and three sequential losses that he experienced brought forth from Cabot a smile born of wit and wisdom, "You know Dad, I should never have played you again."

The one other game that I remember vividly as being a most important part of my youth was the board game "Risk." Whoever designed this game was an absolute genius. It is a game of world domination, a game where success depends on three things: strategy, daring (risk), and the throw of the dice. The latter is the most frustrating part of the game because one has absolutely no control as to how the numbers turn up, but strategy and daring could be learned and learn we did. Five or six of us would congregate in Denny Richardson's house and play this game for hours, nay days, nay weeks, and I am very serious about the durations. Denny had sent away for extra armies, so that it was possible to amass phenomenal defenses at the borders of continents, defenses that would have put the Maginot Line to shame. And oh, how we learned our geography. Imagine a 12-year-old boy knowing the whereabouts of Yakutsk, Irkutsk, or Kamchatka! And we all learned, too, that North America and Asia were the best places to occupy and control, North America because it could only be attacked from three places and Asia because of its tremendous mass. On every turn one received five extra armies for owning North America and seven for Asia, even before having to throw the dice. For securing Europe, one received five extra armies as well, but we discovered all too soon that Europe is "The Graveyard," or at least that's what we called it. It just had too many borders, making it susceptible to invasion from multiple directions. How true that is. In playing this game we also learned the power of making alliances, as well as the fragility of those alliances once personal interests were at stake. There were always risks involved in managing this game and to the lads who gathered to play it day after day the lessons were as valuable as most that we were to learn later in life. With that said, reality did creep into this incubator of learning one day. I can still remember when Jack Clark received a phone call that took him away from the table. His sister Judy had been hit by a car in crossing Rt. 20. She died the next day, and for some reason the game of Risk no longer seemed so important to us.

Games were critical to my childhood, and although I could give many other examples of what I enjoyed and the lessons learned, let me move on to sport, which to me was perhaps even more important in my growth, because it developed both mind and body. If I talk sport, I must bring my father into the picture. Unlike Uncle Bernard, Dad did not have an interest in games. He played darts and table tennis with us (and was pretty darn good!), and he always went bowling with Uncle Bernard and me, but board games seemed foolish to him. Sport, however, was another matter. There were no TVs around to speak of in 1949 when my parents and sister came to America, but my father would seek one out at the local bar for what he always referred to as "Friday Night Fights." Dad was not a pugilist in any sense of the word, but he did love to see a good boxer. He disliked Muhammad Ali as a man (too much of a braggart), but he had nothing but praise for him as a boxer, the best he had seen. He never encouraged me to box, and I'm glad that he did not, because all in all he was a gentle man and discouraged fighting.

Dad was not around all that much when I was a child, or so it seemed to me. He was a scale mechanic working for Toledo Scales, and that job kept him on the move throughout New York State. Plus, when he was home it seemed like he was always sleeping, and when he wasn't doing that, he was outside doing yard work, which I've always hated. But something happened in my eighth year of life—I joined a Little League Baseball team, McEwan Coal and Oil. This was the minor league, appropriate for my age level, and Chainyk Builders was the major league team, to which I aspired. Our colors were black and white, which we wore proudly. I don't know how it happened, but I ended up with a round glove and was put behind the plate. After a few practices my father heard Head Coach Gizotti say, in reference to me, "Nothing gets by him." My father's chest grew two inches at that moment, and he was forever after my greatest fan. I don't believe he ever missed a baseball practice, and he certainly never missed a game. I was selected for the All-Star Team that first season and then moved up to the majors. Once there, I sat warming the bench, as the Assistant Coach's son was a catcher also; another life lesson learned.

I hung up my baseball glove after three years, as I got tired of bench warming. Plus, it was getting in the way of other summer activities, such as our going to Lake George as a family. Some of the best times of my life occurred at Lake George, especially in those years between ages 15 and 17, but back to sport. If you are around a lake, your first priority is to learn how to swim. I did have an idea of such since age seven, but swimming skills were especially honed at around age 12. If you wanted to waterski or drive a boat, you had to know how to swim well, so I, along with many others at our trailer camp, took numerous swimming lessons. I learned how to do every stroke (crawl, breast, and side) and I was, by far, the ugliest swimmer on Lake George. My arms, legs, and head went in all sorts of contrary directions as I swam, but I did have one positive that was an advantage. I either won, placed, or showed in every race I was in, much to the chagrin of my various instructors. I didn't care what I looked like as long as I got to the finish rope first and, as time went by, more often than not I walked away with ribbons or trophies, a time when such mementos were not given simply for participation. One race that I always won was distance under water. Almost by intuition I knew that you don't need your arms in underwater swimming; in fact, they get in the way. I would put them by my side and, in torpedo fashion, kick my legs like the devil and plow ahead at uncanny speeds. It helped having calves like Popeye's arms, an attribute that also fared me well in the game of soccer.

Soccer was my sport. It wasn't my favorite sport, but it was the sport that I excelled in. For two years I was Co-Captain of the Junior Varsity at Guilderland High School and in my senior year I was Co-Captain of the Varsity. In the three years that I played in high school the only games that we lost was the first game I played and the last game, with the last one sadly denying us a New York State regional championship. I was recruited at several colleges but went instead to Harvard where I was but a small pea in a big pod that consisted of several players who had already served on their national Olympic teams. I did play freshman soccer (and again, my father traveled to Boston to watch every game), but I just wasn't in the same league with my mates and I knew that my skills were better served at Eliot House than in collegiate play. I was player-coach for

Eliot House and in three years of play we never lost a game, even when we played the champion college team (equivalent to houses) at Yale at the end of each year. Thus, my record stands at but two losses in seven years of play.

In the years while Cabot was growing up, I served in a voluntary fashion as an assistant coach to various YMCA and club soccer teams, and for 10 years I was the head coach. I even have a professional soccer license, but only because it was required of me in order to continue coaching club soccer. In the final year of my coaching, when Cabot was a senior in high school, the Tuscaloosa Rowdies (I inherited the club and its name) went to the State championship, and lost by one goal—the story of my life. Cabot was not recruited by any university, as he hadn't done "Olympic Development," but he did try out with 125 other students for Syracuse University's sole club team. There were only four or five positions to fill and, much to my happiness, he was selected. I went to see him play at Syracuse and was bowled over by his skills. In every sport he more than surpassed my abilities, and I am very proud of him for that. I can still beat him at chess, but that's neither here nor there.[15]

Basketball. That's my game and always will be. I loved it from the first time I ever bounced that big orange ball and, had I been four inches taller, my life would have been very different, or at least I like to think so. Bob MacDowell and I just barely made the B team in 8th grade. And then, in 9th grade, we just barely made the freshman team. And then, in 10th grade we just barely made the JV team. I can still remember inching up to the board outside the locker room after each practice to see if I was still on the list. Never have I experienced such joy to see my name on that board week after week until finally each team was set. By my last year in high school Bob and I were the only seniors left on the Varsity squad, the

---

15 Correction—Christmas 2020 we played again. The match ended in a stalemate.

only difference being that Bob, at six-feet-four-inches, was the Captain and I was second string, the same position that I held in the violin section of orchestra. I only started one or two games in Varsity basketball and did not distinguish myself, by any means. In fact, I still have this dream of Coach McAvoy walking slowly toward me at the end of one of our games when I took a buzzer shot instead of passing it to Bob, as per his instructions. He never reaches me in my dream, but I can still see those red eyes penetrating to my very core. Bob went on to play basketball at Hobart College and, in his senior year, was their Captain. I went on to play intramural basketball at Harvard and helped Eliot House have a decent if not distinguished record each year. Also at Harvard I played a fairly good game of squash and helped Eliot House with that as well. In my senior year I was the Athletic Secretary for my house, a paid position, and we won the Straus Cup that year.

Thus ends my life with sport. I played a little squash in Graduate School but have never played on any soccer or basketball team in the years since college. I never really miss doing so, as I had had my day, but I have continued to be a fan of basketball all my life. I have been a season ticket holder since coming to the University of Alabama, which helps explain why we can never seem to advance much in the post season. Basketball is not only a jinx for me, but it is also a jinx for any team I have supported (save the Celtics). However, if the University of Alabama ever gets a men's soccer team, my presence will stand them in good stead, of that I guarantee.

We the People, We the TV

TV IN THE MID TWENTIETH CENTURY WAS A LIMITING EXPERIENCE, as there really was not much out there. My favorite shows in the 1950s, in the general order of my maturity, were "Howdy Doody," "I Love Lucy," "Walt Disney Presents," "Leave it to Beaver," "The Donna Reed Show," "The Twilight Zone," "The Honeymooners," and "Dobie Gillis." I should add to this as well "The Lawrence Welk Show," which might seem strange. My mother was a die-hard fan of Lawrence Welk and so there was no option for any of us who failed to flee the living room when it came on the air. It did result in eight years of violin playing for me, so that at least gratified my mother as to the educational qualities of television. And it also, I presume, gave her great pleasure—little for me admittedly, and absolutely none for my sister, as Jennifer hated the screeching (often done intentionally) of my practicing. For the 1960s, I would have to go with "The Flintstones," "Maverick," "Dick Van Dyke," "Get Smart," "All in the Family," "Laugh In," "The Smothers Brothers," and "Peyton Place" (again, mother-inspired). I always preferred the sit-coms, westerns to some extent but never cops, doctors, or lawyers.

The thing about the 1950s and 1960s is that we really had no options. You watched one of three channels, ABC, CBS, or NBC, and sometimes only two if the bunny ears were not working right. When PBS arrived, it was akin to a miracle, but my TV tastes were already well defined by then so it did not have as much appeal as it might have had in my developmental history. Every child, every normal child, looked forward with great anticipation to that day in September (or was it even as early as August?) when all the new shows were announced. How sad we were when some of these attractions overlapped. Without the ability to tape shows, some heartfelt decisions were in order, and lord help you if you had a sibling who wanted to watch other things. I knew of no one who had more than one TV in their homes and anyone who had a color TV was the friend of choice, despite the eerie reds and greens that were constantly being adjusted to preferences. The new shows that were announced in September were on the three network schedules for the whole year, not just for five or six weeks as they are now. And it is good that weekly viewing numbers did not affect their existence, because some great shows really did take a while to gain an audience. I remember groaning whenever Jack Kelly substituted for James Garner as Maverick, but the more that I saw him the more I came to like him. And when their English cousin Beau appeared, I thought, "well here's a guy who might have a future."[16] In short, TV tastes were cultivated by familiarity. The characters increasingly became our friends, but as with most friendships the attachments do not occur right away. Today producers are far too impatient to have sponsorship money rolling in, so I suspect that a lot of true gems have been lost to the TV viewing world.

Once I got to college my TV watching started to flounder, as would be expected. Henry Moreta, my roommate and I did watch "Dark Shadows" (sadly), "Jeopardy," "Sanford and Son," and "Bill Cosby," and we always tuned into "The Tonight Show," just to see what Johnny was up to. Once I got into graduate school, however, I didn't even have access to a TV, so that

---

16 Roger Moore of course went on to fame in "The Saint" and as one of the personifications of James Bond.

was that. By the time the late 1970s rolled around my TV viewing diminished even more, but no longer was it because it was not available. I was married by then and we did have a small TV (black and white), but the shows that I watched were minimal and they generally had already been around for a few seasons. Consequently, when I did start watching them they were already tried and true. These included "Mary Tyler Moore," "Barney Miller," "Newhart," "Taxi," and "Carol Burnett." Shows that I'm pretty sure that I watched from the beginning during the 1980s were "Tracy Ullman," which included the Simpsons when they were truly ugly and despicable, "Night Court," "Soap," and "Cheers."

By the time I got into the 1990s, the number of shows that I watched regularly had diminished even more. "Seinfeld" we always watched, and generally as a family. "3rd Rock from the Sun" was another favorite, as was "Friends," but the highlight for me was "Everybody Loves Raymond"—but wasn't that the 2000s? This thing called "time" is a very depressing concept. Easty and I did not discover "The Big Bang Theory" in the 2010s until it was already around for three or four seasons. Whoever came up with that title is deserving of being drawn and quartered because it certainly never drew us in. In fact, it pushed us away! We only stumbled into watching this show by accident, but in doing so we rapidly came to the realization that it did indeed have high quality. I should say "does," as the BBT is still underway, but either our personal tastes have altered or the show has played itself out, because we no longer are fans.

For the last decade there really has been very little on TV that has garnered my interest beyond the "The Big Bang Theory," "The Office," and "Curb Your Enthusiasm," but before leaving this testimonial I should mention that there have been some series that have lured me in over the years. Masterpiece Theatre was always a draw for me, with special favorites being "The Forsyte Saga," "Upstairs, Downstairs," "Downton Abbey," "Victoria," and "The Durrells in Corfu." Plus, I must admit that Easty and I were "Dallas" fanatics for a time, she more than me, and "American Idol" addicts, she most definitely more than me. This mindless and endless extravaganza lost its appeal to me right after my wife's obsession with Adam Lambert replaced her obsession with Elvis. Now, beyond a sporting event per week (but none during the pandemic), I really only watch the News. Never has TV News been so important to me as it was during the Trump presidency and its after effects, because now when they say "Breaking News," it really is true. Because it is breaking each and every day, I am drawn to the tube mainly to make sure that there will indeed be another day. The Chinese curse has finally come into fruition for TV viewers, "May you live in interesting times."

Expectations of Movies

"Badges? We don't need no stinking badges!"
"What could happen to an Old Fashioned?"
"Hump? What hump?"
These are some of the lines that I have used over the years in a multitude of contexts. There are dozens more. Some stimulus will occur, and I reach back into my memory of experience to draw out the appropriate line. When my children eventually saw "Young Frankenstein" (1974), they looked at Easty and me in amazement, "So that's where all those expressions came from!" Film is a medium that we take for granted, but its characters, messages and one-liners seep into our subconscious in ways that are difficult to recognize or understand. What follows in this essay are stream of consciousness thoughts on the impact of movies on my life. I prefer to do it this way rather than to make a list, because I feel that if the films really are important to me, they will rise to the surface like cream as I write. I expect a certain amount of structure must exist in me so as to draw thoughts from my gray matter and guide my fingers. With that said, the process is different when I use a pen, in the fashion of my diary, than when I type directly into the computer, as I am doing now. There is no possibility for revising once ink is applied to paper, but for the word processor there is ample opportunity for revision, and I do take advantage of such. With this as a preliminary, let me "press on with all possible dispatch."[17]

---

17   So as to quote Terry Thomas in "It's a Mad Mad Mad Mad World" (1963).

I defy anyone alive today to know with precision the first movie they ever saw. "Remember" yes, but "saw" is another issue. This was not the case for our parents, as movies really were an anomaly when they were young. For most people alive today, however, exposure to cine has existed from birth and has always been a part of our lives. I suppose that my first film would have been at a drive-in theater, as we didn't have a TV until I was four or five. The last thing my parents would have tolerated was a rude child at an indoor theater asking loudly, "What did he say?" At a drive-in theater they could easily relegate me to the back seat with strict instructions to go to sleep and, as a child, I always took instructions well. The first movie that I recollect seeing at a theater is "Friendly Persuasion" (1956). My mother had already viewed it and thought I would be enamored with a little Amish boy being chased across the lawn by the family's pet goose and sticking his tongue out in derision once he had escaped. She was right. I thought it was the funniest thing I had ever seen and, as I was only five at the time, that may be true. What I remember most about the film was its phenomenal musical score by Dmitri Tiomkin (I still have the record and continue to be enchanted by its melodies) and by the dilemma the family faced when confronted by war. I have seen this movie many times over the years and, what with its all-star cast (Gary Cooper, Dorothy McGuire, and Anthony Perkins), it has held up very well. Another Cooper movie that had an impact on me, though I didn't see it until much later, was "Sargent York" (1941) which, quite coincidentally, is an anti-war movie as well. Perhaps conscientious objector is a more fitting description than anti-war, as York does eventually do the "right" thing and fight for the "right" reason. As stated in an earlier essay (see p. 45), "Gone with the Wind" (1939) is another film that pressed upon my mind. There is not a battle in the film, but there are certainly a lot of dead and dying bodies. I will never forget the Atlanta scene when Scarlet is exposed to the victims of Sherman's army all laid out before her, hundreds and hundreds of moaning souls. Movies like these started me on the road of wondering why warfare is so universal, a topic that has been a question for me all my life and has been the subject of some of my teaching. I have walked many a battlefield and sat before many a gun placement in my time. Easty would drop me off and pick me up several hours later...most times. For years she doubted my sanity, but she finally understood my infatuation with places where men shed blood when I explained to her that it is not because I glamorize war; I am simply trying to understand why men do this crazy thing and revel in it. She still has occasion to doubt my sanity of course, but at least it is not because of my interest in warfare.

In my youth I had great expectations of movies. In addition to making me reflect upon such matters as man's violence to man and scaring me half to death with notions of death (the coach bearing a headless horseman in "Darby O'Gill and the Little People" 1959, almost did me in), film has also given me an appreciation of humor. My tastes range from the purely slapstick (Buster Keaton, Three Stooges, etc.) to the cerebral, though I gained more of an appreciation of the latter as I aged. There is nothing funnier in film to my way of thinking than the mirror scene in the Marx Brothers "Duck Soup" (1933). I gasped for breath when I initially saw it as a young lad and I can remember like it was yesterday when my son saw it for the first time. I watched him carefully as the skit developed and will never forget the expansion of his eyes, the gape of his mouth, and the absolute exhilaration he experienced at the end of the scene. I knew from that very moment that Cabot had humor in his life and that he would be alright. A movie that has become a cult film for our family is "It's a Mad Mad Mad Mad World"

(1963). I don't remember it being so funny when first I saw it at the theater, but it grew with me in time and Easty and I generally have at least one annual showing of it. I suspect we know every line. Good films become old friends.

Those of my generation are of an age when musicals were part of growing up, whether we liked it or not. The two musicals that I waited anxiously for each year, which were always on television at a regularly scheduled time, were "Peter Pan" (always at Christmas) and "The Wizard of Oz" (always at Easter). There was much hubbub in school in the weeks leading up to these showings and lord help the poor child who happened to miss the events. My favorite was "Peter Pan" and the marvelous Mary Martin. The wires were clearly visible, but they faded into my imagination, as I'm sure they did with most children—at least those who believed! In 2009 I happened to be in London by myself and did a lot of walking about the city. While wandering through Kensington Garden one day, I came across a massive tent before which was a poster. That night they were doing a showing of J. M. Barrie's masterpiece within that very tent. I bought my ticket, as this was a performance not to be missed. Imagine, watching "Peter Pan" while actually being in Kensington Gardens! it was indeed a grand performance, bordering as much on trapeze artistry as acting. American that I am, I stood and applauded, the only person to do so (Brits are a strange lot) and, in return, I received a bow from Peter Pan himself. Small favors exchanged.

Every afternoon when I was young the "Early Show" came on at around 4 p.m. This was not the TV series that aired between 1999 and 2012; rather, it was merely a platform for showing movies to kids who just couldn't get enough Cowboys and Indians. Thus, each and every day I saw a black and white film, as they inevitably were. It did not matter, though, because my parents didn't own a color TV until well after I left home for college. As a result of the Early Show, I can truthfully say that I have seen every Grade B western that was ever made, including all of Randolph Scott's productions, but for the life of me I cannot remember a single title. I saw a lot of the 1930s and 1940s classics as well, the Gilded Age of Hollywood, and absorbed them like a sponge. Whether it be "College Bowl" or "Jeopardy" (had it existed at the time), I would have been the victor for anything relating to movies when I was in my teen years.

Time has erased all of that useless information now, so I am squeezing my mind to remember anything that had a significant impact on me in the very late 1950s through1960s. Movies that do stand out to some extent are "Some Like it Hot" (1959), "Tunes of Glory" (1960), "Lawrence of Arabia" (1962), "The Miracle Worker" (1962), "The Music Man" (1962), "To Kill a Mockingbird" (1962), "Lord of the Flies" (1963), "Becket" (1964), "Doctor Zhivago" (1965), "The Graduate" (1967), "Lion in Winter" (1968), and "2001 a Space Odyssey" (1968). There are several films that we were required to see in high school purely for our edification, and which actually did turn out to serve that purpose, as they have indeed left their mark—"David and Lisa" (1962), "The Loneliness of the Long Distance Runner" (1962) and "Seven Angry Men" (1955, but I didn't see it until the mid 1960s).

In college, between 1969 and 1973, my roommate of four years (Henry Moreta) was also a film buff and together we saw more movies than either of us would care to admit, and always with considerable discussion thereafter as to meaning and value. We would take the Red Line and head over to the Publix Theater in downtown Boston. Long since closed, this "grind-run theater on the lower end of Washington Street"[18] (I love that description) offered both old and fairly new films for less than a dollar viewing. The theater also of-

---

18 http://cinematreasures.org/theaters/6405.

fered other things for slightly more than a dollar, but Henry and I managed to stave off these unwanted overtures by sitting in adjacent seats. Movies seen at the Publix and at other establishments in Boston's theater district that immediately come to mind are "Burn" (1969), "Midnight Cowboy" (1969), "The Damned" (1969), "The Sterile Cuckoo" (1969), "Lovers and Other Strangers" (1970), "The Ruling Class" (1972), and any Woody Allen movie that happen to come along. I realize, too, that I have not referred to Paul Neuman, Jack Nicholson, or Michael Caine movies and only one Brando film thus far, which is reprehensible as I enjoyed them all.

As for movies that actually had an impact on me, those days passed with the early 1970s, about the same time that I decided not to pursue an acting career. Despite performing throughout my teen years, both in school and with city institutions (Albany Civic Theater and SUNY Albany), I had to make a choice as to whether the stage or perhaps even stardom in the movies, would be my vocation. At Harvard I acted main stage in 1972 at the Loeb theater ("Johnny Johnson" 1936, an anti-WWI musical) and also produced and acted in two plays at Eliot House ("Witness for the Prosecution" in 1970 and "Peter Pan" in 1973, but not the musical, and no wires!). As the years went by, however, I realized that acting was merely role-playing and with each role played I found I was losing a little bit of myself. I always remember Peter Sellers standing at the podium giving thanks for some award he had received. As the applause wound down and he started to talk, he was plain and uninteresting, a pale shadow of his movie roles. The audience was increasingly uncomfortable and so, quite clearly, was he. Things changed markedly, however, when he donned the accent of Inspector Clouseau from the "Pink Panther" series. As he shifted into that role and others (like Dr. Strangelove) the audience recognized him once more; an ensemble, a hodgepodge of characters made famous by his various manifestations. But who was Peter Sellers? Chauncey Gardiner in "Being There" (1979) ironically may have captured the real Sellers. No one could believe that anyone so simple and gray, as to personality and interests, could be anything but great. In actuality, the real Peter Sellers was the man behind the camera, both literally and figuratively. In real life he could usually be found following others around with a home movie camera at his eye. I didn't want to become that man. Instead, I went into archaeology and simply disappeared behind the scenes.

Since the mid-1970s I have seen a myriad of movies. I have sat through and been bored to death by one "Star Wars" adventure after another and one each of the "Lord of the Rings" and "Harry Potter" fantasy series. I have never been curious enough to see the others. "Raiders of the Lost Ark" (1981) I thought was great, but the sequels paled in comparison, as do most action films that have been released in the last 40 years. It is for the same reason that Bond movies failed to interest me once Sean Connery was no longer in the main role. And yes, I did like "Superman" (the first one with Christopher Reeve, 1978) and "Batman" (the first one with Michael Keaton, 1989), and I even liked my share of modern-day screwy musicals ("Tommy" 1975, "Saturday Night Fever" 1977, "Grease" 1978, and "Chicago" 2002), but very few films have touched me in the last few decades. Those that come to mind, without dredging deeply for others are "Life is Beautiful" (1998), "American Beauty" (1999), and "A Beautiful Mind" (2001). Three films with "beauty" in their titles certainly must say something about me (!), but what I like most about these three films and about movies overall is creativity and originality. I appreciate something that is out of the usual, whether in acting, directing, or producing; something wherein a risk was involved.

"McCabe and Mrs. Miller" (1971) did this for me when I was in college, but it has not held up well over the years.

There is always danger in returning to movies that once were so great to you. Times change, and so do we. Other movies that struck a chord with me at the time that I saw them, yet may not do so now are "In the Heat of the Night"(1965), "True Grit" (the 1969 version with John Wayne), "The Deer Hunter" (1978), "The Sixth Sense" (1999), and "Cold Mountain" (2003). It depresses me that I cannot recollect any since 2003, but probably will do so once my fingers are lifted from these keys. So be it. Movies were dominant in my past, so-so in my present, and maybe obsolete in my future. Despite this depressing note, I must add that all I have to say to a member of my family is "And this old bag...", "Put the candle back..." or "So!" and it causes an immediate and expected reaction. The expectations are based on shared experiences and maybe, in the long run, that's what movies are really meant to be.

Life's Incidentals

(THE DRIVE-IN THEATER, THE CIRCUS, AND THE FAIR)

The Drive-In Theater

I read somewhere that the drive-in theater might be making a comeback. In this time of pandemic when people want desperately to get outside and desire seeing movies on the large screen, yet cannot congregate in groups, it makes sense to reopen these vestiges of the 20th century. The trouble is that so many of the drive-ins have followed the course of the dodo—they are extinct.

How can this be? As a child one of the things that I looked forward to most was going to the Turnpike Drive-In. It was located on Western Avenue in the Town of Guilderland fairly close to my home, although at the time I thought it was located far out in the wilderness. It was built in 1952, a year after my birth, so we were young together it seems. A typical family venture was as follows. My father never was one to move quickly, so at about 6 p.m. on a summer evening Jennifer and I would be pestering him to get on with it. Eventually my mother would gather us into the car to await his emergence from the house. It would have been sunny and hot all day, but every window on the ground floor had to be closed, because of rain he would say, but we all knew that my father was simply locking up his castle. We were never robbed in our lives, probably because there was not a thief in existence in our suburban neighborhood, but my Dad would have attributed our good fortune solely to his vigilance.

Once in the car and moving, we would get to the drive-in in about 10 minutes, thereabouts. We always seemed to park in the middle of the grounds and there always was just enough daylight for us to run to the playground and burn off some energy before the cartoons came on. The playground had the usual swings and see-saws, but the device that we all gravitated to was the merry-go-round platform that rotated in either direction as slow or fast as one wished. There were bars to hold on to, but that didn't help much because older imps decided their mission in life was to eject everyone off the disk. More than once I would return to the car filthy, nauseous, beat up, and with a resolution to never do that again, until the next time of course.

All playground activity stopped once the screen lit up. Immediately a squadron of children raced back to their respective cars. I'm sure that Mom, Dad, Jennifer and I sat in the front seat, as that was possible in the 1950s, and with plenty of room to spare. If it was warm enough, we sat outside but that didn't last too long. It was summer and there were mosquitos, so they would drive us inside. Few bugs actually followed us because the smoke from my father's cigarettes discouraged such pests. As my father was a chain smoker and my mother a firm believer that open windows caused drafts detrimental to children's health, we seldom had to worry about bugs. Society knew no better back then.

After a couple of shorts, Mighty Mouse, Mickey Mouse, or some other rodent, the first show would begin. In those days there were always two movies, so a drive-in adventure would last on the order of at least four hours. The first movie tended to be a western, and that was okay with me, especially if John Wayne was in it. What could be better than Cowboys and Indians for a five or six-year-old on a pleasant summer night? There must have been an intermission during the first movie, because we always had a snack. I don't know what my sister had, but for me it was either a fudgsicle or an ice cream sandwich, and usually the latter. All the kids in the lot would race to the white-washed cinderblock building in the middle of the grounds while dancing hot dogs and popcorn boxes filled the screen. My father was happy with his cup of hot coffee, which mystified me then, as it does now.

Once everyone was settled in, with napkins firmly wrapped around the various treats, we watched the end of the movie. As it came to a close, Jennifer and I would sit absolutely still so as not to draw attention to ourselves. That strategy failed, as Mom would eventually say, "Okay, off to bed you two." Despite anguish and complaints, I always succumbed to the demand, but Jennifer only pretended to doze off and was soon up and watching. There was no way my sister would ever sleep if action was about, but I was pretty much putty and did what I was told. An hour or so later the sound would go off and I would wake up, sort of. My father would put the speaker back on the pole and we would then wait for the bulk of the people to clear out. My father was never one to beat the rush, and I suppose I get that from him. He was content to wait and wait and wait, and my mother quietly festered, at least sometimes she did so quietly. She knew who she married but was not always good with it.

For at least the first decade of my life the drive-in theater was an institution. I don't remember my father ever going to an indoor cinema. "Too much mucking about," he would say, which basically meant you had to be there on time. Moreover, some people weren't crazy about you smoking. Plus, you had to pay for individual tickets! At a drive-in theater you paid by the carload, which is about the only time I think that my Dad wished he had more children.

A strange thing happened in the mid to late 1960s—the drive-in theater started to lose its attraction. It may have been because of changes in indoor cinemas. When I was young the latter were simply large palatial theaters that had once catered to Vaudeville. In Albany they had names such as Palace, Strand, or Ritz, and ritzy they were, or at least they once were. All had been converted to movie theaters by the mid-century and by the late 1960s new ones were being created that had all sorts of technological gadgetry. Drive-ins simply could not compete with that wizardry, and yet they did persist for a while.

As a teenager who had not yet reached an age to drive a car, but was too old to be seen with parents, I still liked drive-ins. One day Bob MacDowell, Mike Havern, and I snuck into a different drive-in theater located farther west in Guilderland, whose name now escapes me. We must have walked or hitch-hiked there, which amazes me, but that's what kids did in the 1960s. In any event, as the movie began, we settled ourselves into a central part of the lot, all three of us in a row, and proceeded to enjoy the film. Eventually we were accosted by a young man with a flashlight who questioned our lack of vehicle. "Oh, we're with the car back there and are just sitting up here enjoying the evening." He seemed to accept that but insisted we go back to the car in question in order to verify our story. Just as we were about to reach the vehicle we split up and ran in different directions. Bob and I remained fairly close together as we tumbled into a ravine, but Mike was nowhere to be seen. As the dust cleared, we assessed the damages. There were no broken bones and the guard had not followed us, so we believed ourselves to be safe. Any normal persons would have gone home, but we were teenagers—so back we went. This time we chose a remote part of the lot and kept a watchful eye out for the guard. We were not watchful enough, however, as he eventually returned and grabbed us. "Why did you come back?!" he demanded, to which we meekly responded,

"Because we wanted to see the movie." This time he held on to each of us firmly and delivered us to the main guard at the entrance. The latter pointed to a piece of paper on the wall that had all of our names on it. We were stunned. We got away with a warning and a promise to never come back or there would be police involved. To this day Mike says he never got caught nor gave our names, but Bob and I have always known better.

My next experiences with drive-in theaters were in the late 1960s and early 1970s and by this time I actually had a car! I cannot tell you the name of any movies I saw, because all I really remember are the dates involved; in short, the best movies I have ever not seen! I did notice at around this time, however, that the quality of the movies was going downhill. Unless you were near summer resorts (which I was—at Lake George, New York), drive-in movies that I would see with my peripheral vision from the road tended to be of the seedier sort. They weren't pornographic, at least not yet, but they certainly were trending in that direction. That, I believe, was the death knell of drive-ins. People just didn't want to take their kids to see movies of that sort and, as a result of the burst in popularity of malls, indoor cinemas were blossoming everywhere. By the 1980s and 1990s the big screen of the drive-ins started to come down and with it a part of my youth died.

When my own children were young, it dawned on me that they were missing out on this great part of Americana. Thus, one time when we were visiting my parents who were wintering in the Tampa Bay area, Easty and I decided to take the kids to a place that self-billed as "The Last Drive-In Theater in Florida." That may have been an exaggeration, but it is true there were not many around. Avery and Cabot were not at all enamored in having to see a movie on an outdoor screen and so resisted any attempts on our part to excite them. I parked our car on the front row and then waited patiently for the damn sun to set as the children moaned and groaned. I arranged chairs at the front of our car and all four of us sat there silently peeving. Until my dying day I will remember the look in their eyes when the screen came to life. The movie was "Aladdin" and the voice was Robin Williams', but the star of the show was the big screen and the grand outdoors. To my kids it was absolutely magical, and though I was happy for them, I knew that this was just a blip in their existence. For me it was one of the incidentals of my life.

The Circus

A few years ago when I was flying to London alone on our 40th wedding anniversary (don't ask!) a young woman sat across the aisle from me. Several times in crossing the Atlantic passengers necessarily stretch in their own particular fashion. Her fashion was first to direct one leg and then the other straight up in the air and then draw them close to her body. In short, she resembled a closed clasp knife, an absolute marvel to see. As the lights went on and we prepared to disembark the plane, I could not help but ask her just how she was able to turn herself into a human pretzel? I know I was bordering on sexual harassment, but there was no way I was going to take that mystery to the grave. It turned out she was a trainer of circus acrobats and was on her way to London to teach a class. With the lights up I could see that she was not quite as young as I had presumed, a clear example of how exercise extends youthful appearance, at least in the dark. I marveled at her agility, but later wondered about the future of her trade. After all, the circus was defunct, or at least that was the case in the United States. I was not sure of the rest of the world and still don't know.

Quite coincidentally, my first experience with an actual circus was also in England. In 1959, at the age of seven, I visited my English relatives, meeting most of them for the first time. They primarily resided in Lancaster and Morecambe along the northwest coast of the country. An afternoon trip one day took us to Heysham Head, which is located on the northern tip of Morecambe Bay. There we came across a circus tent and were beckoned in. At a breaking point in the various daredevil events, out came the clown. For some inane thing he planned to do, he needed a helper. A child would do, so he went around the periphery in search of a willing subject. From the perspective of a shy child, which is what I was, he simply needed a victim. I probably stood out like a sore thumb, Yank that I was. Once he made eye contact with me, he walked over, extended his thumb, and dabbed my nose red. Everyone was amused; well, just about everyone.

I don't like clowns. I don't think they are funny and I never have. This may be due to the View-Master that I had as a child, the implement that provided stereoscopic images of various scenes of life. We had one disk that contained multiple images of the Big Top of a large circus, with all the scenes being very dark. Whenever the clowns popped up, they would scare the absolute crap out of me. Thus, I did not take kindly to having my nose rubbed red by this English clown. Even more disconcerting and much to my chagrin, he paraded me around the circle while awaiting the appearance of the acrobats. Or maybe he was killing time before the arrival of lions, horses, bears, or other quadrupeds that were designed to run around in circles simply for the awe and amusement of audiences.

I have never been drawn to a three-ring circus (of any sort!) simply because I get no joy in anticipating someone falling or being eaten. I was not brought up to delight in such misfortunes. This is, I believe, why I have no interest in gymnastics. It's basically the same as the circus except that the participants receive points as they march from one horrifying back-breaking event to the next. Anything going around in circles is an absolute bore to me. Many of my childhood friends had great fun watching little race cars go around and around on tracks of various dimensions, but not me. I just didn't get it. NASCAR is basically equivalent except that periodically a vehicle will come crashing into the crowd and wipe out a few fans. In short, a circus—"The lions are loose!"

I must have gone to a circus or two at some time in the United States, but I just can't remember when exactly. If I did, it would have been in Albany's Washington Avenue Armory, as that was the only indoor arena large enough to support the Ringling Brothers Circus or whatever it was called in the 1950s and 1960s when I was a child. Despite its actual name, it was always billed as The Greatest Show on Earth! To some that may have been so, but not to me. Even Irwin Allen's highly acclaimed movie, "The Big Circus" (1959) was disappointing. David Nelson, of "Ozzie and Harriet" fame was in it, so that was a draw that got me into the theater but having him turn out to be the villain pretty much matched my expectations for circuses.

Back to the clowns. As stated, I don't much care for them and never will. They are smothered in make-up and whether they are smiling or not they are just plain scary. Mimes are not much better. In fact, they are worse, but with that said, my most memorable and positive experience with a mime occurred in New Orleans many years ago. Easty and I were walking down one of the streets all by our lonesome, except for a solitary mime coming our way. "Don't make eye contact," I said, "and he won't bother us." I don't know why I ever bother saying such things to Easty. She delights in people of any ilk and if someone crosses her path with a desire to amuse, she's fair game to participate. And amuse he did. He bounced around us with abandon looking sad at one point and happy the next. He stepped out in front of me and then he moved to my back and copied my gait. He was an absolute pain in the ass. I tried to ignore him. I frowned. I waved him away. I rushed ahead to leave him in the dust, but he just wouldn't let us be. Easty, of course, was beside herself with laughter. Eventually he stopped all his cavorting as I faded into the distance, at which time he looked Easty straight in the eye, and said, "What the hell is the matter with him!?" I turned around and laughed. I had made a mime talk! Now that was funny. I believe I may even have given him a tip, but maybe not.

And The Fair

Many years ago Ben Windham, columnist for the *Tuscaloosa News*, wrote an article on the local Jaycee Fair. I always liked Ben's essays, but this one especially I enjoyed because of its haunting ending. As he wandered the grounds and took in the ambience, his mind started to drift into the past as to what the fair meant in bygone days. At the end, as he was leaving, whatever it was that he had just about grasped, he lost. The Jaycee Fair has long since ended, but I'm glad that my children got to experience it. I did with them what my parents did with me. First things first was to see the animals—the cows, the sheep, the goats, the horses, and whatever other critters one might expect to find on an American farm; not the farm of today perhaps, but certainly of the mid 20th century and earlier. As a child I wondered why my parents did that to my sister and me. We certainly didn't request it because our prime goal was to get to the rides, where the action was. The fair, after all, came but once a year and we had only one night to take it all in.

Let me go back to those times. My first memory of a fair was The Punkintown Fair, located in Voorheesville, New York. This tiny community is located just outside of Albany along the edge of the Heldebergs, a large escarpment to the west of where I lived. I "Googled" the fair up and discovered that it held its 77th anniversary in 2019, so it started in 1942, just nine years before I was born. I'm embarrassed to say, however, that I always thought it was called "Pumpkin Town" because it occurred in the fall and there were always truckloads of pumpkins scattered about. Now it is held in July, which is not exactly the harvest season, and that perhaps may be why the name changed, if it actually did. Then again, it could be due to the innocence of a child who mixes up words and hears what he wants to hear. I, for example, always ended my prayers with, "Pity mice and pity me," only to learn as an adult that it was supposed to be, "Pity my simplicity." So, it remains Pumpkin Town Fair to me!

The big fair for the region was the Altamont Fair. It occurs each year in the little village of Altamont, but it caters to the people of Albany, Greene and Schenectady counties. Altamont, which means "High Mountain," was originally part of an early 17th-century Dutch manor in what eventually became the town of Guilderland. By the end of the 19th century Altamont was a summer vacation spot that was reached by train. The Altamont Fair started in 1893 and continues strong today. In my memory, it always occurred the third week of August, just after my birthday. Going to the fair was equivalent to the best birthday party a kid could ever have. Things remembered, after the animals that is, are cotton candy, carnival barkers, little plastic ducks swirling around in water tanks, stuffed animals that were next to impossible to win, stodgy rough-looking men bearing cheap, smelly cigars in their mouths, candied apples, and ride upon ride, most of which were too old for me and off limits. The one that I loved and continued to love into my early adult years was the Tilt-A-Whirl. This ride had seven cars that twirled around in unpredictable ways, as the platform upon which they were fastened went up and down in a wave-like fashion. if you could manage to get on one with a fat kid your car would swing with abandon and create just the right amount of dizziness. It was wonderful.

Usually when we left the Altamont Fair, totally spent from all the activities and weighted down with useless crap, we would go through an area filled with items that had won awards. Someone's peach pie had a first-place ribbon in the made-from-scratch pie category, and innumerable 4-H awards went to kids who grew the largest tomato or squash or figured out a new mousetrap. These were farm kids. I recognized some of the names because I went to school with them but had no idea at the time what this 4-H thing was about. I know now that the purpose of this club, represented by a four-leaf clover symbol, was designed to motivate farm children to be innovative. Their parents and grandparents were suspicious of new-fangled ideas coming out of schools, so the future depended on the children. It's hard to blame the old folk. For centuries, nay millennia, farmers were doing just fine. Assuming the rain was neither too much nor too little, they could feed themselves. Moreover, they could take their excess foods and crafts to the fair to exchange with others for things they so desired. They could also listen to some music, do a little dancing, watch a horse race or two, and eat some ice cream or cotton candy. That's what it's all about. I guess I must have realized all along that was the case, as I made sure that my own children first walked by the animals and last walked by the farm awards. But somehow that meaning does not seem all that relevant today. I guess whatever it was that I figured out by going to the fair, like Ben, I too lost it there.

Music and Not Me

I WOULD LIKE TO SAY THAT MUSIC HAS PLAYED A MAJOR ROLE IN MY life. I would also like to say that playing the violin for eight years has left me with a life-long love of classical music. I would like to say such things so as not to appear a complete dolt, but these would be lies and there is far too much lying going on in our society at present. Thus, I present nothing but the truth here, despite the fact that the truth won't set me free.

There was never any music in my house when I was growing up, or at least there was no background music. My mother was often singing while she worked and, thank God, she did have a pretty voice, but I'm talking more in terms of phonograph or radio. Except for when we were in the car, we as a family did not listen to music. My father carried a small portable radio with him to work that he would periodically turn on at home, but this was used more for news than for music, and even then, it was turned on only sporadically. My older sister, three years my senior, had a 45-rpm record player that we used for children's music, including one of Kukla, Fran, and Ollie that scared the Bajesus out of me. When Jennifer graduated to a 33-rpm phonograph, it was off limits for my use.

I think it bothered my mother that we did not have music in our lives, especially as she loved to hear pianists and often spoke of Chopin as her favorite. Unfortunately, buying records and the technology that went with it were not within our family budget. I can still remember how happy she was (or maybe it was just me?) when the opportunity arose for a used piano coming into our home. One of our neighbors was leaving the area and their piano was ours if we wished. I can still see it being lugged up to the side door of our house. It was too wide to go in straight, but the men doing the lugging, one of whom was my father, thought that if they could turn it just right, they could wiggle it in. They couldn't and my father sure was not about to remove a door and its framework, so off it was wheeled, along with any possibility of me becoming a concert pianist. In hindsight, had my mother really wanted it I think it would have become ours, but c'est la vie. I suspect my sister must have expressed a sigh of relief, but little did she realize at the time that she would soon be tortured by her little brother practicing violin lessons. As stated earlier (see p. 81), the Lawrence Welk Show stimulated me to opt for that instrument when I had choices in third grade. My mother was so delighted, and largely because I hated to disappoint her, I stayed with that instrument through my senior year. When the orchestra leader learned that I would not be playing it in college, she said, "Well, at least you will always have classical music in your life." She was wrong. I really was not a string person. I was jealous of Jack Clark, a boy who I grew up with, as he played the trumpet. Moreover, he got to play in the band, which looked like a heck of a lot more fun than the orchestra to me. I loved musicals. "The Music Man" was my favorite, not only because I lusted after Shirley Jones, but because of the exciting sounds of brass. And later, when I performed in "Gypsy" and was the lights apprentice for "Pajama Game" at the Albany Civic Theater, I realized that I had taken a very wrong direction in musical endeavors.

So, what then does appeal to me in music? I like the sounds of the 1940s and 1950s, the crooners and the bands that backed them up. The Big Band era is the epitome of music for me, so I was definitely not a child of my generation. My wife constantly reminds me of this, as my preferences are her horrors. When we listen to music, and she does so far more than me, we listen within our respective private studies. We don't have background music in the more "public" areas of our home, and we didn't even do so when our kids were growing up. Consequently, and lo and behold, music is not all that important in their lives either. It is certainly shameful for me as a parent to admit that I neither promoted nor encouraged music in Avery's and Cabot's development, but then again, they never have had the guilt of playing an instrument for what seemed like an eternity simply in order to satisfy a parent.

The Point of Dancing

MY PARENTS WERE INCREDIBLE BALLROOM DANCERS. TO MY MOTHER Fred Astaire was a god and Ginger Rogers a goddess. Mom reminded me that Ginger did all the same moves as Fred but did them backwards, and in high heels. A highlight of her life was watching Ginger Rogers dance at the Washington Avenue Armory. My father never talked about dancing or dancers, but when the music began at any event, he would take my mother's hand and head for the floor. Together they whirled around the room as if they were walking on air. They never spoke or even looked at each other, each lost in their own worlds. The crowd would eventually move to the side simply to watch my mother and father perform.

My older sister was quite a dancer as well. Because she came of age in the late 1950s/early 1960s, there were a variety of dances and she knew them all. This was mostly due to her watching "American Bandstand" religiously, something that was never of interest to me. Each time my mother walked by the TV, she would point at the girl with the mountain of teased hair and state, most emphatically, "That girl's going to have biddies!" And sure enough she did, because the report was that she disappeared one day and had to have her head shaved. How the hell do I remember such things?

By the time I was in junior high, the only dances that we did were the Twist, the Mashed Potatoes, and slow dancing. I was very good at the first two and every boy worth his salt was good at slow dancing because all you had to do was hug the girl and shuffle your feet. As long as I had the voluptuous Valerie Hobson at my side, I won every Twist contest. I sadly discovered that she was the key to that success the one time that she danced with another lad. That was okay, though, as slow dancing with Valerie, or Sue, or Mary was the only thing I really wanted to do anyway! This of course continued into high school and into college, but here's where philosophy comes in. The whole point of dancing, at least to me, is to make contact with the torso of your chosen partner, without her calling the cops. Hence, dancing defined. Now, if said person is already agreeable to doing that, well then, what is the point of dancing? Music just doesn't give me happy feet.

I think I danced with Easty maybe three or four times in my life. The first time was at a wedding for one of her college friends. It took maybe three steps for me to discover that she had a decided propensity for leading, one that she refused to give up on that instance, and forever after. The next time we danced was at our wedding, and only because everyone was waiting for us to start the ritual so that they could perform the same. And the last time we danced was at Avery's wedding. It was not a pretty sight, so I was confused when Easty said, "Well, we did a good job!" I was about to disagree until I realized she was talking about raising our daughter. In that and in most things relating to the worth of our children, Easty took the lead, and I am so glad that she did. They turned out great.

What Foods These Morsels Be![19]

THIS WAS A FAVORITE LINE OF THE LATE WILLIAM G. HAAG, Professor of Anthropology at Louisiana State University and a mentor to me and many others. Not that I ever attended LSU (Lord no!), but Bill was such a major figure in Southeastern archaeology that he affected many of my generation with his wisdom, wit, and bounty. Whenever several of us stayed at his Baton Rouge home, as we often did in the 1970s, Bill would serve us steak, grits, and eggs for breakfast—Southern hospitality at its best. When I think of the South and its people, I always think of food. If you want to be received well, wherever you go in this world, you eat their food, and smile when you're doing so. Otherwise, you'll never get on—and that's a fact!

For this little bit of food philosophy, I owe much to my mother. How often in this book I have reached back into my childhood and addressed the influence my parents had on me, either positively or negatively. From the moment I took my first breath of air I was wrestling for control of my life, a little creature reliant on grown-ups, but with an earnest desire to be free of the pressures of others. Those "others" at first were parents. Most children soon learned what "No!" meant and we also discovered that the things that we put in our mouths were not always best for us. Sugary things were to our liking, so why then must we eat things that are green and boring? To eat or not to eat[20] was probably the first wrestling match that we had

---

19 My apologies to William Shakespeare and his "A Midsummer Night's Dream."
20 Further apologies are offered to the Bard's "The Tragedy of Hamlet."

with the elders who brought us into the world. For me it was a losing battle, though I fought bravely over many a meal in my time.

Each meal in our house was sacred, especially as to its timing. Breakfast occurred whenever we emerged from our beds, lunch was at noon, and dinner was at 6 o'clock, whether or not my father was in his seat. The timing was more important than the presence of my father because, as my mother often said, "Your Dad will be late for his own funeral." "The dinner is getting cold Bill!" she would yell as he headed to the bathroom, but this seldom resulted in him altering his own schedule. If anything, it slowed him down even more, much to the chagrin of his wife who had tried all her life to change him. The children, Jennifer and me, would suffer the brunt of the criticism. "Don't be like your father," would be the warning, followed by, "Now eat your vegetables." We didn't have a dog in our early years, or we would have had a ready-made solution to the disposal of food, but even had we had one my mother's hawk-like eyes would have interpreted correctly the meaning of a wagging canine's tail.

The warning that rings in my mind to this day is, "You're not leaving the table until you've finished everything on your plate." Mom never said this loudly, but she was from Yorkshire and among these unusual people who I love so much, decibel level is not necessary to carry messages. Whatever was said was meant; whatever promises were made, were kept; and I am sure that had I not cleaned my plate in those battles staged so many years ago, I would still be sitting there as a tiny skeleton enshrouded with cobwebs. If my father tried to interfere in these conflicts (because Lancashire men clearly could be twisted—my sister knew how to handle her Dad), the immediate response was, "Mind your business Bill." The raising of children was her business. He was in charge of what went on outside the house and she was responsible for anything that lived and breathed within the house, which also included a sequence of caged birds and, eventually, a dog. The latter was "mine" supposedly, but I wasn't the one who fed him and dogs, being somewhat smarter than people, know the importance of the feeding role.

As the years went by, I learned to eat everything that was put in front of me and, much to my surprise, I learned to like it; even to look forward to it. We always ate at the same place, in the kitchen and together. My father would eventually appear at the table, oblivious to the scornful looks of the woman who sat across from him. I don't remember much in the way of conversation, as food was to be consumed for nourishment, not to enrich social occasions. And when we were done, never more than 20 minutes or so (but we always had dessert) we children were required to ask, "Please may I leave the table?" The judgement as to whether or not we were actually done was my mother's alone, never left up to my sister or me. And so we grew, pound by pound, year by year, into respectable, healthy creatures.

If I have given the impression that meal-time in my early years was akin to a concentration camp, it is only because it seemed that way. The only time I ever really felt that I was in danger was when I was sassing my Mom about something or other and she accidentally dumped a bowl of soup on my head. She apologized profusely and never, even in later years, admitted that there may have been a cause to the slippage. Had she not been a Yorkshire lass who knew the value of a bowl of soup, I would have been very suspicious indeed.

I know this has been a somewhat tedious journey through table manners and the youthful challenges to nutrition, but it sets the stage for food and the rest of my life. It was because I ate everything that was put in front of me in childhood, that

I have never strayed from that practice in post-teen years. When I went to Harvard and had my first meals in the Freshman Union, I was in absolute nirvana. Students to the left and right of me were complaining as if they were straight out of a Dickens novel, but I loved it all. I can still remember the baked beans and codfish cakes, which would turn my wife's stomach were she to read this account. The only foods in college that I was suspicious of were the "soybean chicken" and the "soybean ham." Had they just called it "little soybean squares, sometimes white and sometimes pink," I think I would have been okay with that, but I have never liked food hypocrisy. Tell me what it is, and I will eat it.

I must immediately eat my words, however. When I traveled in China in 1999, which was not my first time abroad, but was my longest episode in foreign lands, I really did not want to know what was put before me.[21] An explanation is in order. I was the oldest person on the archaeological expedition that took place in the Three Gorges region of the Yangtze River and, as a consequence, wherever we went I was always assigned the Elder's chair at the head of the table. Once the dozen or so dishes were ordered by those on the team who were from Sichuan, the contents were always served to me first. As I dipped my chopsticks into the contents, generally laden with small but lethal red peppers, the local people would stare with intensity to observe my reactions. The foods were carefully chosen by them and, as such, it was so important this stranger among them appreciated that fact. Their food, as with all people, is not only their sustenance; it is their life. Because I was well trained at the dinner table and because I was equally well trained at the poker table (thank God for archaeological

---

21 For further discussion of personal gustatory experiences in China, see my *China Memories: Journal of an Archaeologist in the Three Gorges of the Yangtze River in 1999* (New Orleans: University Press of the South, 2019).

fieldwork evenings), my smiles and lip smacking were both believed and appreciated. More often than not, my reactions did indeed match reality, as the food I have eaten in China was absolutely superb. With that said, there were times that I found snakes swimming in my soup and it was not all that unusual for the heads of unidentified creatures to appear on my plate. Thus, my mealtime experiences were challenging. I never made a mistake, though, and not once did I have a soup bowl accidentally spilled on my head. Let me end with that minor victory, as all of this rambling is making me very hungry.

Go East, Old Man

WHEN I WAS A LAD, WE ALWAYS HAD TWO-WEEK VACATIONS. WERE it up to my father, we would never leave the house. He was as slow as molasses and because everything had to be locked down firmly in the home before taking our leave, getting the car in motion was a major enterprise. Hour after hour my sister Jennifer and I would sit in the backseat while my mother groused at my father's many deficiencies when it came to time. "Don't be like your father!" she would warn us, and apparently this admonition sunk in, at least as regards a devotion to time, and not wasting it. Eventually the car and caravan (we always had small trailers) would get rolling and off to the east we would go.

With few exceptions our destination was the ocean. This was always my mother's choice, as those two weeks were hers primarily, and not to be denied. And what the ocean meant to her was a pure vista, unmarred by islands, promontories, or any sign of trees whatsoever. My mother, and my father too, really wanted to be able to see the horizon, as if they were on a ship in the middle of the Atlantic Ocean. Actually being on a ship was an anathema to my mother, as she could not swim and was deathly afraid of water. She was also frightened of heights and even the thought of being in a plane would hospitalize her. Emigrating to America in 1949, a couple of years before I was born must have been a horrendous experience for her, simply because a ship was involved in the process. What a big move this must have been for them as they traveled west to the United States. My parents and sister came from England, the land of their birth, the land of their extended families, and although it was next to impossible for them to return, they at least wanted to look east each summer in the general direction of the British Isles. Thus, our vacation spots tended to be places like Atlantic City, Cape Cod, or Maine.

With the exception of a vacation in central Pennsylvania once or twice (York and Lancaster sounded far too English to them not to check out—over the years I cherished my Amish dolls), we did not travel west in my youth. Even a southerly direction was rare, although we did travel to Florida one Easter and I do recollect visiting Jamestown once. To travel far would have required too much time on the road and that would no doubt have resulted in endless fights between father and mother. One thing about my parents is that they never let peace get in the way of a good argument.

Not until college did I start to expand my interests and at that time I looked both west and south. The extent of "my west" was the Mississippi River. I had read *Huckleberry Finn* and *Life on the Mississippi* and was determined to see that part of the country. Thus, it was with great fortune that my first archaeological fieldwork experience would bring me to the bluffs of western Mississippi, a region that would continue to be the focus of my research interests for the past half century. With the exception of a conference or two in western cities, which could have been anywhere as far as conferences go, I have done very few western sojourns in my life. Memorable ones were leading a three-week lecture tour in the Northwest Coast in 1985, somewhat akin to the blind leading the blind, a brief jaunt to Nebraska in 1989 for an Omaha Indian Powwow, an extended National Historic Landmark meeting in Gallup, New Mexico in 2000, and a Sierra Club service trip to Bandelier National Monument in that same year. Clearly, I am not a poster child for the famous phrase, "Go west, young man." Whether or not Horace Greeley ever actually made this statement is not the issue here—the main point is that he himself stayed in the east too.

In 1989 we did almost move out west in that I was offered a job as Head of the Anthropology Department at the Denver Museum of Natural History. It was a magnificent opportunity and I gave the matter much thought. When I was interviewing for the position, I rented a car and drove all over the countryside to help me decide. I took a jaunt along the Continental Divide, at which time my attention was drawn to a meadow that had several small signs in it. My curiosity was stimulated to the extent that I stopped the car and walked out to see the signs. One said, "Headwaters of the Platte River." I stepped over it to check out the next—"Headwaters of the Republican River;" and on and on. I remember musing upon how strange it was to be standing at the beginnings of such major bodies of water. "And they all head east," I said, and so did I. I left that somewhat intimidating, open, never-ending sky of the American West with no regrets, heading towards the rising sun for trees and security.

I should say that I do appreciate the mountains, the beauty, and the majesty of the west, just as I do all places of natural wonder. I have climbed to the tops of most of the White Mountain peaks in New Hampshire and have skied a goodly number of mountains in New York and Vermont. I love nature and admire and respect the world that I have been placed in. Moreover, as an archaeologist, I have been to places of considerable wildness, even with my own life in peril at times. I would not trade those experiences for anything. However, and with all due apologies to those who look to nature first in their planned travels, I myself look to places that have people in them. Maybe that's the anthropologist in me, but I suspect that it once again is more related to my youth. I remember many a Sunday afternoon jaunt with my parents. We only had one car in the 1950s and Sundays were the only time that my mother actually got to ride in it. At such times, Jennifer and I were packed into the backseat and off we would go. My father mainly liked to see hills and dales, trees and meadows, but after an hour or so of that my mother would lay down the law, "I want to see the villages. I want to see the people." My father saw people every day in his work, as he traveled far afield in upstate New York, but my mother was raising a family in a suburban neighborhood and short of becoming involved in "coffee and gossip groups" (not my mother's cup o' tea), there was not much in the way of life for her beyond the house.

As a youth I went to England once. In 1959, when I was seven years old, we went to Lancaster, my father's natal home, and to nearby Morecambe, where my mother grew up. I met my grandmother and grandfather on my father's side, became reacquainted with my grandfather on my mother's side, and visited with all my aunts, uncles, first cousins, second cousins, and on and on *ad infinitum*. It was wonderful, and perplexing. How was it possible to have so many relatives, so many people who I had never seen before (at least that I could recollect) and who referred to me as "Our Ian, " with the two words flowing endearingly into each other as in "Ourian"? In 1982 I visited England again, this time with my wife of just five years, it being her first time in this land. In Lancaster I met my second cousin (third?) Tom Clare, who was also an archaeologist. My father was there as well, as his mother was in poor shape and he was seeing to her needs. He arranged for Tom to take us on a tour of the countryside to see numerous castles, Roman sites, megalithic monuments, etc. I can remember Dad saying, "Ian is in England for a short time and wants to see everything." I didn't correct him at the time, but what I really wanted to do was to take the time to see some things intensely. I wanted to stay in places long enough to wander, to breath in the air, to see people living their lives. I had no interest in the quick look, checking off this site and that simply to say that I've been there. I have never had a bucket-list of places I want to see and do, and probably never will, but with that said there is a pattern to my wanderings. I have in my later years always looked east, mostly to Europe and primarily to the British Isles. I suppose this is somehow related to those vacations of my youth when both Mom and Dad looked back longingly to all that they had left behind, wondering whether or not they had made the right choice for their children. Exploring the land of my ancestors has helped me understand my roots and though I am not an Englishman and never will be (that I am reminded of every time I travel there), I am enlivened and enriched each time my feet lay upon "this blessed plot, this earth, this realm, this England."[22]

---

22 William Shakespeare, "Richard II."

What Do I Believe?

"WHAT DO I KNOW?" WAS MICHEL DE MONTAIGNE'S FAVORITE SAYING. I like it, mostly because of its ambiguity. Devotees of his could take the phrase to be instructive but Montaigne, with tongue-in-cheek, may merely have been offering a play on words. He could expound on a topic, but then finish with the adage, thus diminishing the value of his exposition. Listen to me or not—I care little. Years ago I wore a button in my lapel at archaeology and museum conferences that said, "What is the Object?" Puzzled looks soon changed to smiles. The usual response was, "I get it Ian," and thus my purpose was achieved.

"What do I Believe?" however, is a different question. It makes me nervous just posing it, largely because this is the first time I am putting forth thoughts on religion in this series of rambling essays. In graduate school I took a course on magic, science, and religion, which also happened to be the title of a book by the famous anthropologist Bronislaw Malinowski.[23] I found that there wasn't a great amount of difference between the three approaches in terms of their goals, but that each assigned emphasis in varying fashions. Philosophers have addressed a myriad of issues over the centuries, but the basic matters are who am I, why am I here, and what happens when

---

23 Malinowski certainly had a way with titles. Only the least inquisitive of budding anthropologists could easily put down his volume on *The Sexual Life of Savages in North-Western Melanesia: an Ethnographic Account of Courtship, Marriage and Family Life among the Natives of the Trobriand Islands, British New Guinea* (London: George Routledge and Sons, Ltd., 1929).

I die? Death is the great equalizer. Everyone is born, a miracle in and of itself, everyone lives, and everyone dies. There are no exceptions. We have a pretty good idea as to why we were born (and it has nothing to do with cabbages!), but as to where we go when we die, that is an enduring mystery. Anyone with gray matter, which actually does resemble cabbages, has thought about these questions, but the vast mass of humanity leaves it to others for acceptable answers—meaning parents, teachers, priests, and coaches.

The child of course puts much trust in the parents, at least at first; I did, but when I found out that Santa Claus did not exist and that he was not responsible for all those toys, I began to question the veracity of my parents. What else did they lie to me about? Christianity should never have paired Jesus's birth with Old St. Nick because when you destroy one icon it's a hard task to maintain the other. I, however, was raised a Methodist and I was virtuous to a T. I learned my Bible, I attended Sunday School, I was a strong advocate of Methodist Youth Fellowship, and I played in the weekly church basketball gatherings at Westmere Elementary School. I did this all through grammar school, as well as during my junior and senior high school years. Even when I got to college, I attended the Harvard-Epworth United Methodist Church services in my freshman year, at least for a while.

On paper I was a good Christian, but I wasn't quite sure I knew what that meant. I did consider myself fortunate, though, to have been born into a family that followed the "one true religion," which is what every child is led to believe. I say family, but what I really mean is my mother. My father felt that church was very important—for kids that is. What was far more important to him, as an adult, was sleeping till noon on Sundays. There was no religion in the world that could convince him that snoozing wasn't a more critical endeavor than sitting in a pew listening to some pundit pontificate as to what God expects of you and what will happen if you don't wake up and pay attention.

Methodists were not of the fire and brimstone sort, at least in my experience, but they were pretty adamant as to what was right and what was wrong, and my minister expected his congregation to follow whatever edicts he put forth. Even as a child I wondered about this. "He's not dead," I mused, "so how does he know what death is like? How does he know that there is a heaven and a hell if he's not been there?" Naturally I kept these thoughts to myself, not wanting to kill yet another Santa by my queries, but still I wondered. Simply resorting to "The Bible says..." did not do it for me but, with that said, I did enjoy the history of the *Old Testament* (some of it at least had to be true), and I appreciated the kindness of the *New Testament*. The lessons of the latter could just as easily be reduced to The Golden Rule, but perhaps this is just the cynic in me talking.

Back to magic, science, and religion. The differences between them can be shown by the following case. A man becomes sick and isn't getting better. The first question he asks is "Why me?" That could be followed up with, "And why not him?" Let's be kind and address just the first question. In the primitive world (if I may be so bold as to use that outdated term), a shaman would be called in. Some taboo may have been broken, so the cure addresses that infraction. If the sickness continues, then witchcraft may be involved. The shaman performs various incantations to remove objects that were injected into the patient. If that too fails, the shaman's power is questioned and his influence in the community is reduced. The witch of course is killed along the way and all is well once more. In science, things have improved somewhat for the case in question. Experimentation has proven that there are germs out there and if one gets into you, the way to rectify it is to take your medicine, but not too much, and not too often, or there will be ramifications. That's because there are other germs out there. You can't see them, but they are there. Modern man accepts this explanation and solution, but the same question still persists, yet in a slightly modified form, "Why did I get the germ and why not him?" We always see ourselves relative to other people because we are social animals; or at least some of us are, with some better than others. Science can provide an explanation for that too, but there are so many numbers and probabilities involved that the common man[24] gets confused, takes the pill, and awaits his destiny. We have unbounded faith in science and scientists, which is really not all that different for more primitive minds having faith in their shamans.

So how does religion enter the equation in dealing with the age-old questions of who we are, why we are here, and where we are going? Mind you, I am no expert on the matter, but from my impression religions are a lot more organized than magicians or scientists. They have their founders, their bibles, their disciples to spread the word, their places of worship and, most importantly, their "we vs. them" holier-than-thou attitudes. You are either part of the team or you are the enemy. There are many rooms in my Father's house to be sure, but there were times that Protestants were not allowed in and times when the doors were shut to Catholics. Jacobites and Whigs fought many a battle over such distinctions, but I find I am rambling.

The main point is that religion as an institution is organized. Things were written down, priestly orders were established, the body and blood of the savior was consumed, for Catholics literally and for Protestants figuratively, and all were told to believe or else! As a child, my mother took every

---

24 My father always referred to "the common man" in discussions when he wished to express what he himself believed.

opportunity available to tell me the stories of the Bible, especially those that had morals to them, and horrors upon horrors if I didn't believe or behave accordingly. But in the back of my mind there were questions. No matter how much I loved my parents, they were mortals, and what do mortals know? As my education continued, I realized that they did not have answers for much of what I was learning beyond grammar school, so why is it that I should accept them as authorities when it came to religion? My minister was trained in the facts and had answers for just about everything, but belief without proof was weighing me down. Surely the same kind of attitude must have prevailed for a Paiute Indian boy who had the audacity to ask why a shaman was using a sucking tube to remove a blood clot from his body. If you are going to be a member of a society, any society, you must believe. At most times in the past those who questioned were put to the torch—but that doesn't mean they were wrong.

So what then do I believe? Do I believe in God? Yes. Note that I did not say "a God." In the Greek and Roman worlds they had a plethora of gods, some more powerful than others, but all played various roles in either championing their favorites or destroying those who did them wrong. This is far too complex for me. I believe in one God that is playing with the universe. "Playing" seems unkind, but I don't intend it to be so. What I mean by it is that mankind has been put here for a purpose (oh, I'm so sorry Darwin), but that the purpose is not divine. The original title for Dante's masterpiece was *Comedy*. I like that better than *Divine Comedy* for some reason. There is not a plan to God's actions, but there is a purpose. In short, the process is more important than the goal. In Steinbeck's *East of Eden* the Hebrew word "timshel" is discussed. It means "Thou mayest"—basically, that although there is an expectation for the course of your life (the path your soul will take), you do have choices. This is of course the Adam and Eve syndrome, because you do not have to follow the plan as laid out. I know in my own life there were several times when I was given a choice to decide, which I knew at the time would create a different trajectory to my existence. In each case I was warned in a supernatural fashion as to whether or not I wished to pursue such a course. Twice I ignored the warnings and I suffered the consequences from practicing free will, but in the long run there were positive effects, largely due to how I handled life afterwards. I know all this sounds mystical, and it is, but I have come to know in my long life on this earth that there are things that logical reasoning cannot explain, and I am fine with that. I have had many choices in my life and often wonder "what if?"

Although raised a Methodist, I am not a Christian. I believe Jesus existed and that he was a good person. I'll give him that, but I do not consider him to be the son of God, our lord and savior, any more than I myself am the son of God. I certainly do not put myself on his level, as he was a very good man, and he also had disciples and a later adherent called Paul to spread his word. I also have no plans to be crucified, though if I keep writing in this vein that could possibly be my destiny. Although drawn to no organized religion, I must emphasize that I do believe in God and hope upon hope that he believes in me. I also believe in guardian spirits. I have one that has saved me, both physically and spiritually (mainly morally) in a myriad of circumstances. There are too many strange things that have happened in my life in the past and that continue to happen now, that a guardian spirit is the only explanation, at least for me. I guess that is part of the reason why the personal Native American belief systems have always appealed to me.

To summarize, if not conclude, I know no more than any other mortal as to who I am, why I am here, or where I am going, but I can at least offer my thoughts, sketchy as they are. I believe each of us has a soul. I accept the general Eskimo belief[25] that when a person dies his or her soul drifts and enters the body of a newborn child (let's call it reincarnation). Eskimos believe it to be a local person, because that was their world, but I believe that the soul, or whatever this essence is, can go anywhere. There may be reasons why the soul does not drift. Instead, it stays in place, sometimes for a short while and sometimes for an eternity. These are "ghosts," pure and simple or, to the more religiously minded, perhaps "spirits" is a better term. I do believe in ghosts—there I admit it—because I have experienced things in my lifetime that can only be attributed to these apparitions. I have written in great length about these events in my daily diary over the past five decades, but very few people have read what I have written. In one case my wife has strictly forbidden my even sharing it! I have extracted these experiences from diary form, typed them up and placed them in my file cabinets—all as unpublished manuscripts. I make no apologies for them because to my way of thinking there are no rational explanations for the events unless one believes in ghosts, guardian spirits, and God, all of which I do. If Catholics can believe in the Father, the Son, and the Holy Ghost, I can be forgiven for not being a true scientist. I'm English after all, so I do have an excuse. The country of my ancestors is teeming with ghosts. I never go looking for them, but I'm often having to come to terms with them, more often as I age—and I do wish that this was not the case.

---

25 I speak here of beliefs prior to when missionaries got involved.

Easty, Avery, and Cabot

This chapter has been difficult for me. When my wife read an earlier draft of the book she asked a question that hit me to the core. "What about us, your family?" My immediate response was "That's several books in the making." Usually I am not at a loss for words, especially written words, but having to summarize my family in a short essay simply stumped me. I could have argued that Easty, Avery, and Cabot appear in numerous places throughout these rambling essays, but as this would have sounded too much like Hamlet's *Rosencrantz and Guildenstern* (and we all know how that ended up!), I felt it better to remain silent and work on it. Four months passed and I still hadn't written a word. "The next rainy day" I told myself and though many such days did occur, the sun eventually appeared and the dogs needed walking. Why is it that this essay has been so difficult to write?

I think my main problem is that I now have 128 daily diaries bearing thousands upon thousands of adventures involving spouse and children, all carefully indexed. For Easty, however, I don't believe I have ever put her name in a diary index because she's listed on just about every page. This bothered her once when she discovered her absence, and although I explained it well (I think), it might be to my advantage to someday go back and simply add to each volume, "Easty Lambert-Brown pp. 1-230." On the subject of diaries, I wish I could go back through them all and carefully pull out all those tender little stories that make family life so treasured, but that I fear would necessitate more time than I have left in life. So, in lieu of that, I shall offer here a stream of consciousness of what my immediate family means to me, offered more in the form of a memoir than a history.

Easty started off in my life as Nancy Lambert. I was drawn to her from the moment I saw her in the spring of 1974 and, 53 years later, I am still drawn to that beautiful woman who has stood by my side so long. Once when we were newlyweds and living on Avery Island we joined up with coworkers at a New Iberia bowling alley. At one point in between turns she asked me to look around and point out who I thought was the most attractive woman in the building. For some reason, "Danger, Danger Will Robinson" flashed through my mind. I'm not sure what it was that stimulated this query, but I did as I was told. The place was packed with beauty, but my eyes returned to my beloved. "There is no one here who attracts me more than you do," I said, and I truly meant it. Paul Newman was once asked how he avoided infidelity in the acting world? As he was married to the inordinately talented and beautiful Joanne Woodward, his response was immediate, "I have steak at home. Why should I go out for hamburger?" I have always felt the same, though I suspect that Nancy, now called Easty, might have felt she got stuck with ground beef on occasion.

Easty and I first got to know each other in the field while working on a Harvard project located north of Vicksburg, Mississippi. In those days the field seasons were long, almost three months in duration, but I have never experienced a shorter summer. For the next three years Easty and I were geographically separated, as I was in Rhode Island and she was in Massachusetts and later in New Jersey, but we somehow managed to get together on a fairly regular basis and our romance continued to blossom. In 1977 we were wed. New Jersey has a funny rule about marriage though. It seems that a woman's last name automatically changes to that of her husband, or at least it did in 1977, so not long after our marital bonds were forged, we were back at the courthouse getting her name back. Now that might seem a strange thing to do right after a honeymoon, but I can assure the reader that I was good with it. Lambert-Brown was not only a far classier handle than Nancy Brown, but over the years I have had considerable amusement witnessing people coming to terms with hyphenations and the like and with Easty having to do the explaining. The Easty name was a bit harder for me to handle, not because I disliked it, but because when you have spent almost five decades referring to the love of your life as Nancy, it's a little hard to change gears. I did though because I know how much the Easty name means to her. It's a family name and a story for another time.

Not long after we were married, Easty and I moved to Avery Island in southwest Louisiana where we lived for two years. We loved this island paradise and we loved the people there, but life was not easy because of the isolation. Easty was (and still is) very gregarious, much more of a city girl than country, and accustomed to having lots of friends. As our closest neighbors on Avery Island were alligators, the environment did not sit well with Easty and it started to affect her health. Our lives changed dramatically when we acquired a kitten, something to care for. Tchula was our first child. Between her "crazy hour" each night and her occasional all-night escapades as she matured, she severely tested our parental skills, but she was our baby and she helped us get through the usual pitfalls that occur in the first few years of marriage.

When we moved to Watertown in 1979 Tchula came with us and became a northern cat, though she never took to snow. Both Easty and I worked at the Peabody Museum, she as a graphic illustrator for the Institute of Conservation Archaeology and me as a Research Associate for the Lower Mississippi

Survey. Our position titles at the Peabody changed as the years went by, but we continued to live in Watertown for 11 years, changing houses only once. Many friends came to visit us during this interval, as the Boston area is a magnet for such, and we ourselves made several good friendships that have lasted a lifetime. Moreover, we increasingly got to know each other and realized the value of what we had. Five years into our marriage we started talking about having children. It may seem strange, but I don't remember even addressing the topic of children until we had been together for eight years, three pre-marriage and five post. I'm not sure what that means, but I suspect that the catalyst for Avery, our first child, was due to three reasons: 1) it looked like our marriage was going to last; 2) Grandparents were starting to ask nosy questions; and 3) friends were starting to pop out babies left and right.

Once Easty learned she was pregnant, we were both absolutely delighted. For many months both our house and our behavior went into "baby mode." All sorts of preparations were necessary for the arrival of offspring and because of Easty's attention to detail, all went according to plan. She had the perfect pregnancy, perfect that is until the very last moment. We got to the hospital a little early because of a false alarm, but instead of returning home, which we should have done in hindsight, the doctor decided he could move things along by inducing the birth. Without going into details, this was a very big mistake. The actual birth took well over 24 hours and there were times during those two days that I thought I was going to lose both my wife and my daughter. It was horrible— and I wasn't even the one having the baby!

Once Avery was born, Avery Lambert Brown that is, the world was bright again. Tchula wasn't too excited about this new creature in the house, but she soon got used to her and managed to keep a good distance away from those increasingly probing hands. For the first months of her life Avery went to work with us each day, swinging between us in her little seat as we scaled the Peabody Museum steps. By this time Easty was the Staff Artist for the Museum and Avery was the celebrity for all those who came by to fetch their drawings. My first recognition that Avery was a real person was a crib event. It was about the time that she discovered how to pull herself up and stand on somewhat shaky legs. Dinshaw Gobhai, the young child of our landlady, who occupied the other half of our duplex, came by to see Avery perform this new skill. Soon bored, he decided to get into the act by pulling his T-shirt over his head and hopping around like a monkey. Although Avery was at first startled by his theatrics, she soon started to giggle. A gentle chuckle soon turned into hysterical laughter and then tears began to stream down her face. I knew right then and there that Avery, our lovely daughter, had a sense of humor and that all would be well in her world. Life always has its ups and downs, but if a person is able to recognize the funny things in life and know how to laugh to maintain balance, life itself will turn out okay.

There were so many other memories with Avery that I don't know where to begin. Tent camping with a constipated two-year-old was one adventure better left unreported (at least here), watching and recording her dance performances through the years, listening to her sing "Oklahoma" in the back seat of the car, carrying her on my shoulders as she picked at "Slimy" on the top of my beret, holding her before the mirror wrapped in a towel after her bath and whispering, "Each peach pear plum" followed by her loud, "No! Each peach pear plum!" or taking her to a burial ground to draw gravestone designs as I recorded inscriptions. What strange things to remember, of little meaning to all but myself, as I doubt that even Avery has much of a recollection; and if she does it is probably merely because I have mentioned them so many times as treasured moments.

Two very vivid memories of Avery that shed light on her personality and character relate to a funeral and a festival. Great Uncle Don Lambert, the last remaining brother of the Lamberts of Houlton, Maine, died when Avery was three or four (again, I'm avoiding a search of diaries). We hesitated to take her to the funeral because we feared how she would react to the somber mood of the gathering or whether she would act up and embarrass us. We needn't have worried. As soon as we entered the funeral home Avery went up to the closed coffin, tapped it, and asked in a gentle voice, "Is he in there?" We indicated he was and that seemed to satisfy her. She sat beside us for a while and then joined Poppy, her grandfather, in a room that happened to be filled with male members of the family. They were sitting in a circle and were very quiet, but that situation had changed radically when Easty and I entered the room 20 minutes later. There was Avery in the center of the group dancing and laughing, and had everyone else laughing too. I myself was born of a generation where death was hidden. My parents never took my sister nor I to a wake or funeral, at least not one that I can remember. This was a mistake I believe, because it is important for children to understand the cycle of life, not to mention that their presence at such events helps older folk cope with the sadness.

Another event that sheds light on Avery's personality occurred at an Indian festival, a powwow, that we attended while still living in Watertown. Dancing is typical at powwows, often competitive dancing, but there are also times when the general public is invited to participate. As soon as the caller announced that a snake dance was next and that everyone could join in, Avery was off and running. She took the hand of the person at the end of the line and happily slithered back and forth around the grounds in rhythm with the music. We knew we were in trouble though when the caller yelled out "Reverse the direction." Suddenly Avery was at the front of the line and was expected to lead the group. Had I been her age and put in such a situation, I would have looked for the nearest snake hole to plunge into, but not Avery. She was in her element. She wound the group around, keeping time to the music, appreciating the crowd, and involving everyone in her perception of the joy of life.

When Cabot came along in 1987, no one could have been happier than Avery—at first. She was so excited when her Mommy and Daddy headed off to the hospital to fetch a baby boy. We left Avery with dear friend Wendy Lurie (known forever as "Window" to our children) and informed Avery that we might not be back for a day or two, knowing from experience just how long babies take to enter the world. Not so. It's taken a while, but I have learned over the years that patience is the only thing that a parent really acquires from experiences gained of raising one child that can be used for raising the next. For everything else, you can throw your knowledge out the window as kids, more often than not, are as different as night and day. Even in the instance of birth, we were absolutely wrong as to our predictions. We were running like mad the moment we got into Brigham and Women's Hospital because Cabot was coming out. He was in a hurry then and that attitude carried over for much of his youth. I know babies are supposed to crawl before they walk, but I don't remember the crawling stage for Cabot. And for that matter, I don't even remember the walking stage! He was always off like a bolt of lightning. The only thing that could slow him down was the Mr. Rogers Show, of all things. It must have been his mesmerizing voice, but whatever it was that did it we appreciated the calming influence.

Once when Cabot was no more than three years old, we vacationed in Canada, eventually making our way to Niagara Falls. I can still see him at one of the campgrounds we stayed at. A lapse of attention on my part and he was off and running. When I finally caught up with him, he had climbed on to an adult bike that was leaning against a tree. His legs couldn't quite reach the pedals, but he was pedaling anyway as fast as he could. This off and running business made us a nervous wreck at Niagara Falls. We decided to put him on an English toddler leash, much to the shock of our fellow Americans. I remain firmly convinced that the leash was the only thing that kept Cabot from going over the falls. Avery told him he had actually gone over the falls, and it was a matter of disappointment to him years later when he found out this was not true. It was also on this trip that a simple restaurant meal almost resulted in our arrest. As we were led to our table, I told our somewhat gaumless waitress to be sure not to put anything in front of the boy at any time during the meal. I guess I didn't make myself plain enough. When the knife hit her squarely in the back, however, I think she finally got the message. Fortunately, as Cabot had not yet honed his athletic skills, she did survive and managed to secure a pretty good tip in the process too.

I was actually worried that Cabot might grow up to be a bully, as he had a habit as a child of prancing around like he was cock of the walk. Soon after the beginning of his first year at the University Place Montessori School in Tuscaloosa I dropped him off at the door one morning. He thought he had left me at the car, but I was actually right behind him and accidentally stood on the back of his shoe. He spun around with a crestfallen look and before realizing who had done this indiscretion he said, "Oh I am so sorry..." Yes, he was a good boy, and I knew we had nothing to worry about. From small things like this you see the man in the boy and the woman in the girl, but oh what a lot of growing pains occur in between.

Avery is four and a half years older than Cabot. This gap was not planned, but it sure came in handy when higher education loomed. We never had to pay for more than one child at a time, but with that said, first we had to get them to college years. There was a possibility that one of them might not make it, simply because he or she was going to kill the other. Despite the age difference, Cabot was quite proficient in driving his sister to absolute distraction. Avery had an ingenious way of coming to terms with these troubles—she would hit him. My method was to take her to the side and gently explain to her that although she sees before her a little boy, said child drinks milk and eventually he won't be so little. Cabot seemingly was okay with the periodic slugs, water off a duck's back so to speak, but one day when he was about eight or so he slugged back. Avery was stunned and I could tell from her face that this new development was not exactly to her liking. Donning my academic mode I said, "See, as I told you many times, someday he would be stronger than you." I could see the gears working as she cogitated over this change in circumstances. She smiled and responded in a slow and methodical voice, "Well, I had my day." She did indeed and, as always, was very adaptable.

As with all children, the years slip by quickly for their parents. Once we moved to Tuscaloosa, the circle of friends for both Avery and Cabot got larger and larger and Easty and I moved increasingly to the edge of their world. Our involvement was strong, good parents as we are (as say we), but I'm not sure that was appreciated by our kids at the time. Easty was heavily involved in PTA and Girl Scouts and I coached soccer for well over a decade and took the kids on numerous Museum Expeditions, to name but a few of the things we did to enjoy, educate, and I suppose often annoy our children. Only when

Avery went off to Stephens College and majored in Theatre did I discover her latent interest in this fine art. Had I recognized this earlier I would have arranged for a litany of season tickets to various thespian establishments, taking her to such with abandon. Perhaps this is why she kept those dreams and ambitions close to her heart. And with Cabot, I was surprised when he elected to pursue Civil Engineering as a career. When he enrolled in the School of Engineering at Syracuse University I really wondered if he might not have found a liberal arts curriculum more to his liking. I was wrong on both accounts, which just goes to show that although we think we know just what makes our children tick, we really don't, and that's okay. More often than not they turn out just fine. All we ever really needed was patience.

2020–The Year of the Pandemic[26]

THE LIKES AND DISLIKES OF 2020.

I taught my last courses at the University of Alabama in the spring, with the months of April and May all in Zoom. I did not like that.

I retired on June 1 after teaching 40 years, 10.5 of which were with the Crimson and 29.5 were with the Crimson Tide. I went out in a fizzle, which was really okay, as t'was the way I came in.

I like that the graduation of my last Ph.D., Clay Nelson, was able to take place despite the pandemic. He walked in August, making him the last of a total of 10 doctorates I advised (for one I was co-chair with Jim Knight). I like that the graduation took place, but dislike that faculty were neither invited nor allowed to attend. It was one of but a handful of graduations I've missed in three decades of teaching in Tuscaloosa.

I do like retirement very much but miss colleagues and students. I still serve on five doctoral committees and one thesis committee, however, so Zooming remains in my future.

I don't miss committees nor administrative work and like being able to say "no" without any sense of guilt.

I like having plenty of time to read and write.

I like living in the historic district of Tuscaloosa with plenty of quiet, isolated places to walk without having to mask up.

---

26 This essay was originally published as "Ian W. Brown," *Teocentli* 124 (2021):22-23. My heartfelt thanks to the editor of this journal for permitting its inclusion in these rambles.

I like spending more time with Easty and our canine children, Gracie and Dugan. They've never had it so good, the dogs that is.

I truly hate having lost four friends this year, none from COVID-19, but lost nevertheless. For one of them I was supposed to give the eulogy, but that was canceled. Instead, and with the help of over 50 of his colleagues, friends and family, I wrote a book—*Richard S. Fuller Southeastern Archaeologist: Warts and All* to honor him.

I like having successfully finished my personal "Franklin Library Project" (see p. 53), but dislike having no more books to read—right! I currently am typing up the six journals of my thoughts on these books, which are all in cursive writing, as I really do think with my pen.

I like bringing my past adventures to fruition, *Behind Glass in Russia 1992: An Archaeologist's Journal* being a 2020 example.

I dislike that I cannot assemble with friends.

I miss Wednesday breakfasts with the Elders (three nationally acclaimed historians and a piddling archaeologist). For the past couple of years we have each composed essays on dozens of topics and circulated them to each other with abandon. Unbeknownst to them (at least at first), I assembled the lot into a massive tome, combining respective essays with the email commentary that went back and forth between the four of us. The final version of that compendium was released in manuscript form in 2020 under the title, "By and For the Elders." By mutual agreement, we decided to neither publish nor distribute this work, thereby emphasizing "For" in the title. I only mention it here because of just how important these ruminations with three dear friends have meant to me. I not only got to know them better, but I got to know myself better. What I like most about having conducted this Boswellian exercise is discovering that despite our different backgrounds and variable personalities, we really do share a lot of commonality simply by growing up in the third quarter of the 20th century.

What I mostly like about 2020 is that it is over. It is perhaps the most memorable year in my life, but as not all memories are good, I am glad to be done with it.

The author with his diary.

A NOTE ON THE TYPE

The text of this book was set in Filosofia, a typeface designed by Zuzana Licko in 1996 as a revival of the typefaces of Giambattista Bodoni (1740-1813). She based her design on the letterpress practice of altering the cut of the letters to match the size for which they were to be used. The chapter heads were set in Sant'Elia Script which was designed by Ryan Martinson and published by Yellow Design Studio in 2015.